Redefined

A Bible, Life, and Word Study for Women

Cyndi Dodson

Published by
Vision Run Publishing
VisionRun.com

Redefined:

A Bible, Life, and Word
Study for Women

Regroup • Rest • Reset • Rearrange • Rem
• Rethink • Realign • Repurpose • Relations
Release • Recollect • Rehearse • Recipe • Re
eal • Revelation • Receive • Restore • Rel
Reaction • Rely • Require • Reshape • Rega
• Remain • Relax • Refuse • Regrow • Rep

Cyndi Dodson

ReDefined: *A Bible, Life, and Word Study for Women*
by Cyndi Dodson

Copyright © October, 2025 by Cyndi Dodson
ISBN 978-1-954509-20-7

For my parents, who planted faith.
For my husband, who encourages it.
For my daughters, who inspire it.
For my family and friends, who live it.
And for every woman, may you know
   what it means to live ReDefined
   by the love of Christ.

Contents

Introduction: Redefined   9
Week 1: Repurpose   16
Week 2: Relationships   20
Week 3: Rejoice   25
Week 4: Rest   29
Week 5: Release   33
Week 6: Regroup   37
Week 7: Remember   42
Week 8: Recollect   46
Week 9: Rehearse   51
Week 10: Recipe   55
Week 11: Reschedule   60
Week 12: Reveal   65
Week 13: Revelation   71
Week 14: Receive   76
Week 15: Restore   81
Week 16: Reliance   86
Week 17: Repair   90
Week 18: Reaction   94
Week 19: Rely   99
Week 20: Require   103
Week 21: Reshape   107
Week 22: Regardless   111
Week 23: Remind   116
Week 24: Resolve   121
Week 25: Remain   126
Week 26: Relax   131
Week 27: Refuse   136
Week 28: Regrow   141

Week 29: Repetition   147
Week 30: Reach   152
Week 31: Re-examine   158
Week 32: Real   163
Week 33: Recognize   168
Week 34: Reverse   173
Week 35: Reflection   179
Week 36: Ready   185
Week 37: Replace   190
Week 38: Rearrange   197
Week 39: Resist   202
Week 40: Recalculate/Recalculating   208
Week 41: Relight   213
Week 42: Review   218
Week 43: Reimagine   223
Week 44: Redo   230
Week 45: Refocus   235
Week 46: Rebreak   240
Week 47: Re-grip   245
Week 48: Renew   251
Week 49: Realize   256
Week 50: Realign   261
Week 51: Reject   266
Week 52: Respite   272
Bonus Weeks: *278*
   Relentless   279
   Refine   283
   Response   287
   Reflect   292
Conclusion   295
About the Author: Cyndi Dodson   298

Introduction
to the study

Re • de-fine'd

10 - Cyndi Dodson

Re • Defined

Growing up, one of my favorite teachers was my fourth-grade teacher, Mrs. Thomas, at Blue Grass Elementary School. She welcomed this bright-eyed, 9-year-old little girl who transferred schools at Christmas of her third-grade year and was still acclimating to the new school. Mrs. Thomas loved the English language and shared that love with her students by emphasizing vocabulary words and definitions. I remember having vocabulary words for homework almost every night. Mrs. Thomas would define new words almost daily with such eloquence and emotion that the words would come alive, nearly jumping off the page. I learned that the words we choose to express our emotions, describe events, or speak to others give our lives meaning. Mrs. Thomas said that our words are our choice, and we should select them wisely because they cannot be unsaid once spoken. These words define our reality, give meaning to our lives, build others up or tear them down, and ultimately determine our path in life. She chose to speak life into her students and, by doing so, helped imbue our impressionable young minds with the ability to see the world around us with a whole new perspective.

The words we choose to speak are ultimately selected based on how we personally define these words. What one word means to you may mean something different altogether to me. For example – how I define family may be completely different from how another person defines it. One definition is not right, while the other definition is wrong. Both definitions can be completely accurate—they are simply different.

When Mrs. Thomas would check our homework in class, she would see that one word would have several definitions. As 4th-grade students in the 1980s, we pre-dated Google and only had a limited number of resources. We used dictionaries, our parents, or in a pinch (if we forgot to do our homework), we would make up definitions right before we turned in our papers. Those were always my favorite responses and I believe, Mrs. Thomas's favorite too. Ultimately, Mrs. Thomas would decide what definition the class would use as the agreed-upon definition.

When it comes to the agreed-upon definition of vocabulary words in our world today, we have a "teacher" who is our ultimate decider. God sets that standard, decides the "winner", and defines the words that shape our world today. At times we want to make up our own definitions or change words to fit our circumstances, but God and His Word define us, our reality, and our vocabulary.

When God's transforming power impacts our lives, our language, and our vocabulary, we are changed so dramatically that everything in our lives is redefined. Everyday words and circumstances, when examined through God's lens, take on a whole new definition. Situations that otherwise would seem inexplicable gain an entirely new meaning when held up to the light of God's definition. With that in mind, this book aims to redefine these "re" words with the filter of God's life-altering ability to transform every aspect of our daily lives with His redefining power.

When we have a life-altering encounter with the ultimate Teacher, and meet Him intimately as Lord and Savior personally, our life radically changes. Jesus is referred to in the Bible as "rabbi" in several passages. Nicodemus, a member of the ruling Jerusalem Sanhedrin, was considered a "teacher himself in Israel" in his own right (John 3:10), and refers to

Jesus as a rabbi. "He came to Jesus at night and said, 'Rabbi, we know you are a teacher who has come from God. For no one could perform the miraculous signs you are doing if God were not with him'," John 3:2.

Jesus is referred to as a teacher or rabbi, and although we may have many teachers in our lives who have had profound effects on us, none of these teachers will ever impact our lives to the extent that Jesus will. Our relationship with Jesus is the most important relationship we will ever have. Jesus as a teacher in our lives is just one of the many roles He will play in our existence. When we truly meet Jesus, and He becomes our Savior, He takes on so many attributes and roles that it becomes difficult to name them all.

Friend, Advocate, Counselor, My Salvation, Comforter, Master, Savior, Provider, Creator, My Deliverer, Shepherd, King, My Strength, Almighty, Father, Rock, Helper, My Hiding Place, Hope, My Portion, The Most Holy, Almighty, My Peace, Way Maker, Most High, My Shield, Redeemer, Great Physician, Lamb of God, Prince of Peace, Light of the World, Promise Keeper, Sustainer, My Exceeding Joy, True Vine, Miracle Worker, Faithful, My Defender, Wonderful, My Dwelling Place, All Sufficient, My Fortress, Blessed, Anointed, Love, All Consuming Fire, My Jesus Christ – "The Alpha & The Omega – The one who is, who was and who is to come!" Revelation 1:8.

Just as Jesus has these amazing and powerful names, when we begin a relationship with Him, He changes our name and redefines our very existence. We are no longer defined by what we have done in our past, who has hurt us, or whom we have allowed to define us. Certain individuals may have labeled us in ways we do not agree with, but Jesus redefines us with His love, forgiveness, and mercy. Jesus takes our past sins and even our future mistakes, sins, and failures and transforms them through His power of forgiveness and redefines us as His dearly loved and chosen friend. Only through receiving His grace can we become redefined as we accept the blood He shed on the cross for us. It is this relationship that redefines us, our vocabulary, our language, and our destination not only in this life but in eternity. When we become redefined, everything around us becomes redefined too.

He takes our brokenness, our pains, our struggles, and the pieces of our lives that we have defined as unusable, ugly, worthless, and trash. He redefines them as beautiful, capable, and functioning pieces that can be purposefully used and then strategically places them in areas of our lives that create magnificent mosaics. When we allow Him to pick up the broken pieces of our lives and strategically reposition them to make these mosaics, we become the masterpieces we were always intended to become — thus redefining our brokenness and becoming redefined in the process.

The purpose of this book is to examine some of the words we use every day and redefine their meanings according to God's definition. He has redefined our personal meaning and purpose according to His worth and value. The way we define our circumstances, our lives, and even our very beings are completely redefined by God's life-altering and transforming power in such a way that our lives will never be the same. Our language, definitions, and vocabulary are forever altered so that we replace our definitions with God's definitions and see ourselves and live our lives through His defining power and not our own – becoming ourselves REDEFINED.

Week
1

Repurpose

Repurpose:

Verb

Definition: to adapt for use in a different way

Synonyms: remodel and save

An entire decorating phenomenon has been created around repurposing everyday items into new, creative, fun projects. A television channel has inspired millions of people to redecorate their homes and convinced them that it is easy, stating they too can include items that are repurposed to make a dramatic impact while being fun in the process. Repurposed items are all around us: old ladders hung on a wall to become a bookshelf, bicycles turned into planters, old window frames used as tabletops, and bathtubs transformed to couches. The sky is the limit. All you need is your imagination to see a particular item and what you can create. What the original item was intended for takes on an entirely new purpose when it is purchased at an estate sale, antique shop, or garage sale. When the item is bought and paid for, the purchaser has an idea of what he or she wants to make with it. While the original purpose was fine, the new creation is highlighted with before and after pictures, and who doesn't love a good before and after transformation? The same can be said about us. God created us in His image and sent His Son to purchase us with His shed blood. This transformation makes us a new creation, repurposed from our old self, increasing our value, and allowing God to use us for His work and for His glory. Our original material remains intact, but we are now upcycled into what God intended for us to become in the first place. We must acknowledge our need to be repurposed and transformed by the purchase of Jesus' shed blood. As repurposed creations, our before and after images are on display for the world to see in hopes they want to be transformed as well.

Daily Scriptures & Questions
Monday

2 Corinthians 5:17 "If any man be in Christ, he is a new creature: old things are passed away; all things become new."

How does being created in God's image shape my identity?

Tuesday

Ephesians 2:10 "For we are God's handiwork, created in Christ Jesus to do good works, which God prepared in advance for us to do."

In what way do I view myself as God's handiwork and masterpiece?

Wednesday

Isaiah 43:19 "See, I am doing a new thing! Now it springs up; do you not perceive it? I am making a way in the wilderness and streams in the wasteland."

What new thing(s) do I see God doing in my life today?

Thursday

Philippians 2:13 "For it is God who works in you to will and to act in order to fulfill His good purpose."

How can I apply this verse to my life today?

Friday

Proverbs 19:21 "You can make many plans, but the Lord's purpose will prevail."

Am I working towards God's purpose or my plans in my life today?

Weekly Wrap Up

Repurpose redefined:

How can I apply this to my daily life?

Week
2

Relationships

Relationships:

Noun

Definition: the way in which two or more concepts, people or objects are connected

Synonyms: association and connection

In life, we have three primary relationships from which everything else flows. According to Luke 10:27, we are to "Love the Lord your God with all your heart and with all your soul and with all your strength and with all your mind and love your neighbor as yourself." We are to love God, others, and ourselves. The focus of this verse is to love God. That relationship is the foundation for all other relationships we will ever have. If we love God the way that this verse describes, then loving our neighbor as ourselves should flow from our love for God. Let's look at who God says are neighbor is and how we should love them. The verse from Luke above is from the parable of the Good Samaritan where Jesus is teaching a lawyer about how to inherit eternal life. Jesus tells him the verse above and then goes on to talk about a man who was robbed, beaten, and left in the ditch on the side of the road to Jericho. He was ignored by a priest, and a Levite passed by him. The only person who stopped to help was a Samaritan. He bandaged his wounds, put him on his animal and took him to an innkeeper, and paid for the innkeeper to care for him in whatever way was needed. In our lives, there are people in ditches all around us. Our "neighbors" need bandaging for their wounds, be they physical, mental, or spiritual. Most just need love and mercy like the Samaritan provided. Some of the hurting people in our lives could be people we work with, go to church with, or even those who live in our own homes. We need relationships in our lives to survive and thrive, but we need to be real, open, and aware that people are hurting and in need all around us.

The point of our relationships is to point people to Jesus, and we can do that by meeting their needs. But we can't ask if the injured person is "one of mine" or how they got in the ditch or why they got there in the first place. The hurting person could be the grocery clerk, the person who makes your coffee, your co-worker or your best friend. It doesn't matter.

We can't think or expect someone else to help them, like the priest and the Levite who passed by and left the injured man in the ditch. God expects us to help. We can't be so busy that we don't make time for others. The Samaritan stopped. Sometimes we just need to make enough time in our busy schedules to allow time for God to work. We need to make time to stop, look around, and see who needs help. The Samaritan who helped probably didn't carry a First Aid Kit, so more than likely he had to rip his own clothes to create bandages to tend to the injured man's wounds. We need to pick others up and carry them when they don't have the strength to carry themselves. When the Samaritan put the injured man on his animal to ride, that meant that the Samaritan had to walk beside him into town. Helping others will cost us something. It will be uncomfortable. Our relationships become redefined when we help others in God's strength and not our own. When we show love, mercy, kindness, and compassion to others we offer healing from a tough and broken world that beats people up and abandons them in ditches, lost and alone. It is in God's strength that we are able to provide the help that pulls them from the ditch, points them to Jesus, and ultimately redefines how we love others, ourselves, and God. We need to ask ourselves regarding the people that we are in a relationship with, are we living in a way that is drawing them closer to God, and am I loving them the way that God has called me to?

Daily Scriptures & Questions:

Monday

Romans 12:10 "Be devoted to one another in love. Honor one another above yourselves."

How can I love those in my life today and honor them above myself?

Tuesday

Ephesians 4:32 "Be kind and compassionate to one another, forgiving each other, just as Christ has forgiven you."

What does forgiveness look like in my life? Who do I need to forgive?

Wednesday

1 Thessalonians 5:11 "Therefore encourage one another to build each other up, just as in fact you are doing."

Who can I encourage today and how?

Thursday

Matthew 7:12 "So in everything, do to others what you would have them to do to you, for this sums up the Law and the Prophets."

How do I live by "The Golden Rule" in my daily life?

Friday

Ephesians 4:2 "Be completely humble and gentle: be patient, bearing with one another in love."

What does it mean to be completely humble and patient with others?

Weekly Wrap Up

Relationships redefined:

How can I apply this to my daily life?

Week
3

Rejoice

Rejoice

Verb

Definition- feel or show great joy or delight

Synonyms – elation, cheer, celebration

Joy differs from happiness. To *re-joice* assumes that we have experienced joy once, so we can now experience it over and over again. Happiness is dependent on our outward, pleasant circumstances. Joy can be experienced no matter what is going on around us and is independent of our earthly situations. Rejoicing is the secret to being content in all things at all times.

The Bible tells us to rejoice always – not tomorrow or when we think our circumstances will change. It's easy to fall into thoughts of, "I'll have joy when..." When I get a better job, I am offered a raise, I get to go on vacation, my husband finally changes, my kids are succeeding (whatever that means), my marriage is peaceful, my health is good, I get out of debt— whatever that "if" or "when" may be. We are called to rejoice always. 1 Thessalonians 5:16-18 tells us to "Rejoice always, pray continually, give thanks in all circumstances; for this is God's will for you in Christ Jesus." This isn't a fake it until you make it kind of joy. This joy is found in God alone and allows us to find our joy in Him causing us to be able to rejoice no matter what. When we truly surrender our all to Him and realize that we are only under the illusion of being in personal control of our lives; we can rejoice in the realization that He holds us in the palm of His hand and all things work together for our good and His glory.

Our joy can't come from our performance as a human, a Christian, an employee, a mom, a wife, or any other title we may hold. We must constantly evaluate where we are seeking to receive our joy. Is it from social media, television, our children, marriage, or our jobs? We must replace these hollow vessels with the only true source of joy—Jesus. Although God created meaningful relationships, projects, and activities (I'm not sure I would include social media) for a valuable purpose in our lives, their true objective was never to replace Him or to be our primary source of joy.

Finally, rejoicing at all times requires that we are joyful even during difficulties or when circumstances do not line up with our expectations. We must admit that God is God, and we are not. Paul wrote Philippians 4:4, "Rejoice in the Lord always. I will say it again: Rejoice," while he was in prison. To say his circumstances weren't ideal is an understatement. Paul knew that his joy wasn't dependent on his situation and trusted God that He knew what He was doing. It's always easier to read about someone else doing it rather than applying it to our own lives, but this is where the "rubber meets the road" as they say. We can't let our struggles define us. Our identity, focus, and purpose need to be in Christ alone. When we rejoice in our struggles it takes the power off of our situation and returns the power back where it belongs – on Jesus. His supreme authority is over every situation whether good or bad and redefines it through His power and might, not our own.

Daily Scriptures & Questions
Monday

Psalm 118:24 "This is the day that the Lord has made; let us rejoice and be glad in it."

How can I rejoice today?

Tuesday

Psalm 37:4 "Delight yourself in the Lord, and He will give you the desires of your heart."

What can I do today to delight myself in the Lord?

Wednesday

Romans 12:12 "Rejoice in hope, be patient in tribulation, be constant in prayer."

How can I live constantly in prayer?

Thursday

Romans 15:13 "May the God of hope fill you with all joy and peace in believing, so that by the power of the Holy Spirit you may abound in hope."

Am I filled with joy and peace by the Holy Spirit's power so I can abound in hope?

Friday

Psalm 40:16 "But may all who seek you rejoice and be glad in you; may those who love your salvation say continually, 'Great is the Lord!'"

Who can I tell today of the Lord's greatness in my life?

Weekly Wrap Up

Rejoice redefined:

How can I apply this to my daily life?

Week
4

Rest

Rest

Verb

Definition- cease work or movement to relax, refresh oneself

Synonyms- pause, relax

I love that God prioritizes rest. It is one of my favorite things to do, maybe too much sometimes. But since God makes it a priority, we should too. God rested on the seventh day (Genesis 2:2-3) after working hard all week creating the earth. Psalm 23:1-2 says "He makes me lie down" but some days He doesn't have to make me. In other seasons in my life, I have had to make rest a priority or it will not happen. We have to prioritize rest, or it will not fit into our busy schedules. If we don't make it a priority, we will burn out or crash from pure exhaustion. Not scheduling times of rest can lead to sickness and mental and physical overload.

We can't effectively do what God has called us to do if we are worn out, burned out, and empty. It may seem selfish, but sometimes we simply need to take time for ourselves before we can give any more to others. It's like the airplane analogy. When the flight attendant on an airplane gives the safety presentation, she always says to put the oxygen mask on yourself first before trying to help anyone around you. If you are depleted and can't breathe, then you can't help anyone else and will be useless to those around you.

Rest also enables us to think more clearly and focus on what is important. What are my priorities? What is God saying to me? Is there any part of my life that needs more or less attention? Instead of being worn out and going through the exhaustive daily routine, build in time for quiet rest. When we schedule times of rest, it enables us to be more effective, efficient, productive, clear-headed, and alert throughout the rest of the week.

Rest also contributes to peace. When we die, the headstone says, "Rest in peace." This death can occur daily, hour by hour, or minute by minute in our lives before we actually pass away. We can rest in His peace every minute of our lives. When we die to ourselves, we rest in His peace knowing that all we need is Jesus. When we come to the end of ourselves and realize that we are and never will be enough – that is true rest. We can never work enough, be good enough, serve enough, give enough, love enough, whatever enough. Only Jesus is enough, and when we rest in the fact that it is not up to us, we die to ourselves; we lay down responsibility for our ambitions, our goals, and our desires, and we live for Him and what He wants to do and accomplish in and through us. In reality, He can never do anything through us until He does a mighty work in us. It is by dying daily that we can rest in His peace and truly live at rest.

Daily Scriptures & Questions
Monday
Exodus 33:14 "The Lord replied, "I will go with you and I will give you rest."

How does it make you feel knowing God is with you and He is always enough?

Tuesday
Psalm 4:8 "In peace I will lie down and sleep, for you alone, Lord make me dwell in safety."

How will you sleep tonight knowing that God allows you dwell in safety?

Wednesday

Matthew 11:28-30 "Come to me, all you who are weary and burdened, and I will give you rest. Take my yoke upon you and learn from me, for I am gentle and humble in heart, and you will find rest for your souls. For my yoke is easy and my burden is light."

Are there any burdens that you need to give to God today and stop trying to carry on your own?

Thursday

Exodus 20:8-10 "Remember the Sabbath day by keeping it holy. Six days you shall labor and do all your work, but the seventh day is a sabbath to the Lord your God. On it you shall not do any work, neither you, nor your son or daughter, nor your male or female servant, nor your animals, nor any foreigner residing in your towns."

Do you truly honor the Sabbath by resting, physically, and emotionally?

Friday

Psalm 62:1-2 "Truly my soul finds rest in God; my salvation comes from him. Truly he is my rock and my salvation; he is my fortress; I will never be shaken."

Reflect on the idea that God is your rock, and you will not be shaken. How will this impact your day, week, and life?

Weekly Wrap Up

Rest redefined:

How can I apply this to my daily life?

Week
5

Release

Release

Verb

Definition – allow something to move and flow freely

Synonyms – let go, unleash

Our words, actions, and reactions can be suppressed at times. There are times that we don't say the things we want to say (and probably shouldn't) and don't say things that we probably should have said. Once said, however, our words cannot be taken back. Just like a rock that has been thrown once it's tossed, it cannot be taken back. The world we live in is like a huge lake. Everywhere you look, people are throwing rocks at each other – the media, social media, politics, in our own homes, at work, our families, and sometimes, even our "friends." Everything we say, do, and react to is a rock that we throw into the lake, whether we like it or not. We cannot help but touch and impact the people around us with our words and actions. And each of those thrown rocks creates ripple effects that spread out to people we may not even know. If you choose to throw rocks of anger, jealousy, bitterness, or hate into the world, then that is what is spread out to others. But if the rock that you choose to throw is full of love, mercy, grace, kindness, and compassion, then the ripple effects of those rocks are endless as well. And the ripple effects that we create eventually make it back to us. So, we must decide what we want to release into the world today and every day. Do we want to release and send out endless ripple effects of hate or love? Unforgiveness or compassion? Mercy or bitterness? You hold the rock in your hand, so the choice is yours.

Daily Scriptures & Questions
Monday

Matthew 7:24-25 "Therefore anyone who hears these words of mine and acts on them, may be compared to a wise man who built his house on the rock. And the rain fell, and the floods came, and the winds blew and slammed against that house; yet it did not fall, for it had been founded on the rock."

How can I not simply be a "hearer" of God's word but also apply it to my life today?

Tuesday

Galatians 6:7 "Do not be deceived: God cannot be mocked. A man reaps what he sows."

What am I sowing in my life and into the people God places in my circle of influence?

Wednesday

Galatians 6:8 NLT "Those who live only to satisfy their own sinful desires will harvest the consequences of decay and death. But those who live to please the Spirit will harvest everlasting life from the Spirit."

How will I live to please the Holy Spirit today rather than my own sinful desires?

Thursday

James 1:19 "My dear brothers and sisters, take note of this: Everyone should be quick to listen, slow to speak, and slow to become angry."

How will I be quick to listen, slow to speak, and slow to become angry in my interactions with others today?

Friday

Ephesians 4:29 "Do not let any unwholesome talk come out of your mouths, but only what is helpful for building others up according to their needs, that it may benefit those who listen."

How will I be aware of my conversations with others today and ensure that I build others up rather than tear them down?

Weekly Wrap Up

Release redefined:

How can I apply this to my daily life?

Week
6

Regroup

Regroup

Verb

Definition – reorganize for renewed activity

Synonyms – reassemble, transform

We are known by the company we keep as well as the company we don't keep. The people we choose to spend our time with influence our thoughts, behaviors, attitudes, and beliefs. People demonstrate their true character by the choices they make or do not make and the people that you are around the most will eventually determine your future. It has been said if you want to see what you will look like in 10 years, take a look at the people that you spend the most time with and you will have a great snapshot. The same can be said about our children as well. Who we allow our children to "do life with" will ultimately decide where and how far they will go in life.

In the Bible, Lot and Abraham had herdsmen who were not getting along and decided to part ways. Abraham gave Lot the first choice of land. Lot saw what seemed to be the most fertile land and selfishly took it for himself, even though the land included the cities of Sodom and Gomorrah. It is easy to make decisions based on what we see rather than praying and trusting God with what is unseen. Lot moved his family to Sodom and didn't consider the ramifications. This city with a population of around 350,000 was incredibly sinful. Lot expected to live in Sodom but not live like Sodom. Lot underestimated the impact of friends on our lives.

As Abraham pleaded with God to spare Sodom, God said He would spare the city if there were ten righteous people there (Genesis 18:32). As we all know the result, God destroyed Sodom but spared Lot, his wife, and their two daughters as long as they didn't look back on the city as they were leaving. Everyone obeyed except Lot's wife who disobeyed and looked back. She was turned into a pillar of salt.

There are times in our lives when we need to regroup. We need to take an inventory of who we are spending time with and who we are allowing to speak into our lives. Who are we allowing to have a front-row seat in our lives? If we view our lives as a theater, we must carefully consider our audience and the seats we give to our attendees. Not everyone deserves a front-row seat. The ones you allow to sit on the front row need to be people who encourage, uplift, speak God's truth, appreciate your God-given gifts and talents, help you grow, feel better when they are around, give you peace of mind, and lead you closer to Jesus. Other attendees need to be loved from the balcony of our lives. It doesn't mean we don't care for them or that we don't help them or pour into their lives. It simply means that when we regroup, we realize that these relationships are better enjoyed from a distance. Even though our lives may be a theater, we don't need their drama. We understand that we are living our lives for an audience of One, the only One who matters. We must also realize the impact of those who sit on the front row of our lives and by giving them that seat, we are allowing them the opportunity to speak into, impact, and shape our future. We must also evaluate whose front row we are sitting on and what impact we are making on their lives. Are we pouring into them? Are we leading them closer to or farther away from the Lord? Taking time to regroup and choosing our front-row attendees can be life-changing, beneficial, challenging, and rewarding but may require some necessary work. In the end, it will be worth the process as you move forward in faith without the fear of looking back.

Daily Scriptures & Questions
Monday

Proverbs 27:17 ESV "Iron sharpens iron, and one man sharpens another."

Who am I sharpening in my life and who am I allowing to sharpen me?

Tuesday

Proverbs 18:24 "One who has unreliable friends soon comes to ruin, but there is a friend who sticks closer than a brother."

Who am I pouring into, mentoring, and drawing closer to Christ?

Wednesday

1 Corinthians 15:33 "Do not be misled: Bad company corrupts good character."

Is there anyone in my life who is negatively influencing me more than I can positively impact them?

Thursday

Proverbs 12:26 "The righteous choose their friends carefully, but the way of the wicked leads them astray."

Reflect on this scripture and take an inventory. Do I need to regroup and consider who I have allowed a front-row seat to my life?

Friday

John 15:13 "No one has greater love than this- that one lays down his life for his friends."

Who do I need to thank for their Godly influence, mentoring, and impact on my life?

Weekly Wrap Up
Regroup redefined:

How can I apply this to my daily life?

Week 7

Remember

Remember

Verb

Definition - to recall or bring to awareness a past experience

Synonyms – relive, memorialize, rehearse, remind

The Disney classic *Finding Nemo* is one of my all-time favorite movies. The primary character in the story, Marlin, is a father fish who swims the ocean in search of his lost son Nemo. During his adventure, Marlin encounters Dory, a sweet blue fish who suffers from short-term memory loss. As soon as Dory is told a fact, detail, or direction, she immediately forgets the information. Even so, she constantly tries to help Marlin and remains upbeat and positive throughout their search. In some ways, I envy Dory. There are times in my life that I would just as soon forget. There are memories that I never want to be reminded of and images of the past that I wish would fade forever.

I began writing this during the global pandemic, during a year that seemed like nothing but riots, anger, strife, sickness, and turmoil. Everywhere I'd turn, I would hear, "Will this year ever end? Can we just forget this ever happened?" It's natural and normal to want to fast-forward through the bad times in our lives and forget all the messy, messed-up days, months, years, or memories. But when we look to God's word and what He has to say about these memories, He calls us to do the opposite. He calls us to remember.

In Deuteronomy, Moses is finally leading God's people to the Promised Land. To say they have been through some messy and messed up times and years would be an understatement. The Israelites have been wandering for many years. But Moses tells them over and over, don't forget! Remember! Deuteronomy 4:9 says, "Only be careful and watch yourselves closely so that you do not forget the things that your eyes have seen or let them fade from your heart as long as you live. Teach them to your children and to their children after them." Moses wants them to remember where they came from, and that God delivered them out of slavery. Moses wants the Israelites to remember that it was God who rescued them from Egypt. He provided manna for them every day when they were hungry. Remembering takes effort. Focusing on the good requires us to be intentional. Remembering God's goodness and His provisions in our lives requires us to actively think about and reflect on our past. We need to deliberately recall the times that He rescued us, faithfully cared for us, and was there for us no matter what. And when we do remember, we need to do so with a thankful and grateful heart, remaining as upbeat and positive as possible, just like Dory. Even though there are memories that we would all like to forget, God was with us in those times too and He uses all things to make us who we are today. We need to remember to remember and remember to thank Him for what He has done and is doing in our lives every day. And as always, just keep swimming.

Daily Scriptures
Monday

Psalm 103:2 "Bless the Lord, O my soul, and forget not all his benefits."
What good things that God has done in my life do I need to remember?

Tuesday

1 Corinthians 11:2 "Now I commend you because you remember me in everything and maintain the traditions even as I delivered them to you."
How can I be more aware of the Holy Spirit's presence in my life today?

Wednesday

1 Corinthians 11:24 "And when he had given thanks, he broke it, and said, 'This is my body which is for you. Do this in remembrance of me.'"
Remembering that Jesus died on the cross for me, how will I live differently today and who will I tell of His love?

Thursday

1 Corinthians 11:25 "In the same way also he took the cup, after supper saying, 'This cup is the new covenant in my blood. Do this as often as you drink it in remembrance of me.'"
Remembering Jesus shed His blood for me, how will this impact my decisions today?

Friday

Psalm 143:5 "I remember the days of old: I meditate on all that you have done; I ponder the work of your hands."
When I recall God's faithfulness in my life, how will this change the way I live today?

Weekly Wrap Up

Remember redefined:

How can I apply this to my daily life?

Week
8

Recollect

Recollect

Verb

Definition – bring back to mind what is lost or scattered, reminisce,

Synonyms – recall, remember

I only collect two things. My family would tell you that I collect many more, but in actuality I collect two things: crosses and Christmas ornaments. When we travel (and my family loves to travel) my favorite things to do are find a cross from that location and a Christmas ornament for our family Christmas tree. My cross-collection hangs on the wall in my prayer closet. It contains almost 30 crosses and is one of my most prized possessions. When I look at this collection or every year when we decorate our Christmas tree, I am reminded of the places my family has traveled and the sweet memories we have made throughout the years. I am able to re-collect God's goodness over the years. I am able to look back and remember the places we have traveled and realize that God was in those locations too.

The same is true in our daily lives as well. On our journey as we travel through this life, we collect trinkets and reminders of places we have been. We go to work, spend Thanksgiving with our family, meet a friend for coffee, or watch a sunset at home with our spouse. In each one of those moments, we collect a knickknack for our collection – our memory collection. An easy way to re-collect or recall these memories is to build an altar in remembrance like Abram did in the Bible.

In Genesis 12, God told Abram (his name had not yet been changed to Abraham) that He would give Abram all the land to his descendants, and right there, in that place where God spoke, Abram built an altar. Abram wanted to remember or recollect what God said. This would not be the only time that Abram built an altar to God to recollect God's goodness and to represent memorable and significant moments in his life. However, building altars all over our house, city or world is not very practical today. A much easier way to recollect significant occasions in our lives is to build or create a recollection or altar jar. It's a simple and easy way to recollect God's profound events that we have the blessing to experience. Take an empty mason jar or an empty box. You can make your altar box or jar as fancy or plain as you want. Every time something amazing or recollection-worthy happens, or you collect a memorable God trinket – write it down and put it in the altar box. This is your personal altar that you build just like Abram built in Genesis and other heroes of faith built throughout the Bible. These little pieces of paper are your crosses or Christmas ornaments from faraway places that help you remember sweet memories in your life. These notes to yourself are ways to help you re-collect all the times that God has been faithful and put them in one place for safekeeping. When we look back and re-read these notes, we have the opportunity to worship and thank God again and again. These notes can help to build our faith during difficult struggles and remind us that God came through in the past. These records can be gentle reminders when we think we remembered something accurately but in actuality the event was slightly different. These collections of memories are reminders of the roads we have traveled, journeys we have made, and places we have visited with God by our side, and they serve as souvenirs from our trips. May our collections grow daily and may we always recollect God's faithfulness.

Daily Scriptures & Questions
Monday
Exodus 17:15 "And Moses built an altar and called the name of it; The Lord is My Banner."

What does it mean to me for the Lord to be my "banner?"

Tuesday
Genesis 35:1 "Arise, go up to Bethel and dwell there. Make an altar there to the God who appeared to you when you fled from your brother Esau."

Recall a time in your life when you experienced the "goodness of God."

Wednesday
Psalm 77:11 "I will remember the deeds of the Lord; yes, I will remember your miracles of long ago."

Have you ever experienced a miracle of God? Do you believe God still performs miracles today?

Thursday
John 14:26 NKJV "But the Helper, the Holy Spirit, whom the Father will send in My name, He will teach you all things, and bring to your remembrance all things that I said to you."

How is the Holy Spirit your personal "helper" in life?

Friday
Isaiah 46: 9 "Remember the former things, those of long ago; I am God, and there is no other; I am God, and there is none like me."

How can remembering the goodness of God from your past help to build your faith for your future?

Weekly Wrap Up

Recollect redefined:

How can I apply this to my daily life?

Week
9

Rehearse

Rehearse

Verb

Definition – mentally prepare or recite

Synonym – practice, recount

When I was a little girl, playing dress up was one of my favorite things to do. My best friend and I would create plays, write scripts, and act out plays for our parents. We would memorize our lines for the big night and hope everything went great. Sometimes the play went on as we prepared and other times one of us would forget our lines. We were forced to make it up as we went and inevitably everyone ended up laughing and enjoying our performances.

As my friend and I grew up, we developed a motto for our lives: "You only live once." We realized that life isn't a dress rehearsal and like the plays we would act out for our parents, we only get one shot at getting it right. We don't get any do-overs. We can choose to wear a mask in our life and play the role of someone else our entire life or we can choose to be an authentic version of ourselves and play the role that God intended for us to play.

The lines we choose to say are also important in the role we play. How we speak to ourselves, whether positively or negatively can greatly impact our lives. When we rehearse our lines and repeat negative scripts over and over, we bring ourselves down, lower our self-esteem, and diminish our ability to move forward in life. But when the script we rehearse is positive, it creates a healthy emotional atmosphere in which we can thrive, grow, and flourish in such a way that God uses us to fulfill the calling He has placed on our lives.

We can also rehearse our troubles and difficulties in our lives. We can relive sins and failures over and over in our minds. When we do this, we experience them multiple times, when in actuality we were only intended to go through them once. We need to turn our trials over to God and not suffer through them repeatedly. His word says, "Come to me, all you who are weary and burdened, and I will give you rest." - Matthew 11:28. If you are tired of wearing a mask and playing a role you were never intended to play, or if you are tired of replaying scenes over and over in your mind that you were meant to only experience once, or if you are burdened with rehearsing a script that devalues your worth, give it all to Jesus. He will give you new lines to rehearse, a new script from His word to learn. When we surrender to His way, we don't need to perform for anyone, pretend to be someone we are not, or rehearse our lines. We simply read His Word, memorize scripture, and rehearse those words in our minds to play the role in life He called us to play: His cherished and favored daughter.

Daily Scriptures:
Monday

Colossians 3:16 NKJV "Let the word of Christ dwell in you richly in all wisdom, teaching and admonishing one another in psalms and hymns and spiritual songs, singing with grace in your hearts to the Lord."

What is a scripture I can memorize today that speaks to a current situation I am experiencing?

Tuesday

Psalm 119:9 "How can a young man keep his ways pure? By guarding it according to your word"

How is the scripture I am memorizing keeping my ways pure and my heart fixed on God?

Wednesday

Joshua 1:8 NKJV "This Book of the Law shall not depart from your mouth, but you shall meditate in it day and night, that you may observe to do according to all that is written in it. For then you will make your way prosperous, and then you will have good success."

What thoughts am I rehearsing? Am I rehearsing God's word or am I rehearsing my own script and thoughts?

Thursday

Romans 15:4 NKJV "For whatever things were written before were written for our learning, that we through the patience and comfort of the Scriptures might have hope."

What am I learning by meditating on God's word? Do I see a difference in my thought life?

Friday

John 8:31-32 NKJV "Then Jesus said to those Jews who believed Him, "If you abide in My word, you are My disciples indeed. And you shall know the truth, and the truth shall make you free."

What does it look like for me to abide in Jesus and how can I do this daily?

Weekly Wrap Up

Rehearse redefined:

How can I apply this to my daily life?

Week
10

Recipe

Recipe

Noun

Definition- a set of instructions for preparing a particular dish, including a list of ingredients

Synonyms- method, approach, strategy

I can't cook. Well let me rephrase that – I can cook, I am just not particularly good at cooking. But I do enjoy watching cooking shows. The cooking challenge shows that pit chefs against each other using obscure ingredients within a minimal amount of time is one of my favorites. But the shows with a beautiful woman in her perfectly ironed apron, poised in an immaculately clean kitchen that has been professionally decorated run a close second. She has all of her ingredients pre-measured, sitting on her pristine countertop, and makes a "to die for" dish that takes hours for an everyday person like me. But in the miracle of television, *voila*, she pulls a completed casserole out of the oven, complete with 3 side dishes and a dessert and looks ready to host a dinner party – all in 30 minutes or less.

Whether or not one can cook boils down (pun very intended) to your definition of cooking and the use of recipes. The chefs who use obscure ingredients in a minimal amount of time to create fabulous dishes are definitely cooking. The beautiful woman standing in the immaculate kitchen with her premeasured ingredients is also cooking. The tie that binds both of these types of chefs have in common is their recipes. All good chefs use recipes. Even the chefs using the obscure ingredients are following some type of recipe when they create their masterpieces. The actual recipe may either be written on paper, or it could be memorized, but some form of ingredient list is followed. And those of us who don't have our own televised cooking show use recipes too. We swap them, share them, use them, and ask each other for them every day. We go to a friend's house for dinner, a friend brings a meal after surgery, and we read recipes on Pinterest. We are always asking each other, "What is your secret ingredient?"

I believe the same is true when we see someone with a little different flavor in life. Their life is seasoned with a little more flare and spice. We know they have something different in their life and we want that recipe in our life too. We want to know what their secret ingredient is. What is the recipe they are following and what are they cooking with that we should be adding to our lives as well? We want to cook up that dish and serve it to our friends and family, but we need to know the recipe so we can follow it and make it for ourselves.

In Matthew 5, Jesus is delivering the Sermon on the Mount. He discusses how we are called to be the salt and the light of the world. Salt is a well-known compound that has several properties including enhancing flavor. As salt enriches the food we eat and gives it flavor, we are called to flavor those around us in such a way that they are better seasoned for having been around us. We are to enhance the flavor of this world. With a little dash of salt, our words can season the world with love, joy, and peace.

Salt has a unique property in that it affects its surroundings without it allowing its surroundings to affect it. If you put salt in water, the water becomes salt water. If you put salt on ice, the ice melts. This idea of affecting our surroundings rather than allowing our environment to affect us is best illustrated in Jon Gordon's book *The Coffee Bean*. I keep this book on my desk alongside a mason jar full of coffee beans to remind me of his illustration. Gordon discusses how we can all find ourselves in hot water from time to time. This hot water or what we see as trials and difficulties in life can test us. We can be like a carrot and allow the hot water to weaken us or make us soft. We can become like an egg and let the hot water make us hard. Or we can be like a coffee bean and discover the power that lies within us to transform our environment. Rather than allowing the difficulties in life to change us, we change the hot water and permeate our surroundings. We take the hot water and create something new and extraordinary. Life's challenges are just an opportunity to make new flavors. And who doesn't love coffee?

Finally, I believe we all have our own unique recipes that we follow every day to make our lives the masterpiece that God intends us to be. My recipe happens to be my life verse. "Rejoice always, pray continually, and give thanks in all circumstances; for this is God's will for you in Christ Jesus." 1 Thesselonians 5:16-18 By living a life that is seasoned with joy, baked in prayer, and flavored with thanksgiving, I hope to enhance the world around me to the point that others ask what my secret ingredient is. And my answer will always be Jesus.

Daily Scriptures
Monday
Proverbs 16:24 "Gracious words are like a honeycomb, sweet to the soul and healing to the body."

When I think of my words, are they sweet and edifying to those around me? If not, what changes do I need to make?

Tuesday
John 15:5 "I am the vine; you are the branches. Whoever abides in me and I in him, he it is that bears much fruit, for apart from me you can do nothing.

How can abiding in Jesus make me more like the coffee bean discussed in Jon Gordon's book, The Coffee Bean*?*

Wednesday

John 14:6 "Jesus said to him, "I am the way, and the truth, and the life. No one comes to the Father except through me.

Am I being salt to the world around me, enhancing the flavor of the world and impacting my surroundings, or allowing my surroundings to impact me? What changes, if any, do I need to make?

Thursday

Psalm 34:8 "Oh, taste and see that the Lord is good! Blessed is the man who takes refuge in him

What is the recipe I follow that makes up life (my life's verse)?

Friday

Matthew 4:4 "But he answered, "It is written, "'Man shall not live by bread alone, but by every word that comes from the mouth of God.'"

How am I speaking life and my life's verse to those I encounter every day?

Weekly Wrap Up

Recipe redefined:

How can I apply this to my daily life?

Week
11

Reschedule

Reschedule

Verb

Definition- plan again according to a different timetable

Synonyms- postpone, suspend, rearrange

I have never been one to believe in coincidences; that things just happen for no apparent reason. I have always been under the impression that things happen for a definite reason, at a certain time for a clear purpose. I also believe that every person is a miracle and that life doesn't just form out of nowhere. Globs of cells don't just mush together haphazardly at a random time in space and boom – you have a human being. Each person is created for a divine purpose born at the perfect time that God has orchestrated for their life. Psalm 139:13 "For you formed me in my inward parts; you covered me in my mother's womb. I will praise you for I am fearfully and wonderfully made." Fearfully in the Hebrew transliteration means "awesome" so when we are created fearfully, we are literally made awesome by God.

My parents had a difficult time conceiving me. It took several years for them to have me, and I am an only child. Other factors contributed to my lack of siblings, such as the fact that I weighed almost 10 pounds at birth and that when I was old enough to speak, I told my parents I did not want a "bwother or sistor." However, it was God's divine timing that I was born when I was; He was preparing and moving everything into place as on a chess board. God moves chess pieces in our lives to the precise place they need to be before certain events can take place. The same is true for you too. You were born at the precise time that God wanted you to be born and the appointed season that He has planned for you. What my parents or others may see as delays, postponements or setbacks are just God's way of resetting our schedule to align with His timing. When we set our pace to fall in step with God's movement, we see how His perfect plan and timing were right all along. When it's God's timing for something to happen, we can't stop it and when it's not His timing, we can't force it to happen.

 Just ask Mary and Martha in the Bible. Their brother Lazarus got sick, and before he died, they called for Jesus to come and help him. Instead of rushing to the scene, Jesus took His time and by the time He arrived, Lazarus had been dead for four days. Martha questions Jesus' timing and says in John 11:21 "Lord, if you had been here, my brother would not have died." How many of us have asked God a similar question? If you had only been here Lord, then I wouldn't have lost my job. If you had been here Lord, then fill in the blank. Then Mary arrives at Lazarus' tomb and asks Jesus the same question. We are not the only ones who have experienced the same feelings of loss and wondering why the delay. Why did Jesus wait? What took Him so long to show up? Was it because Jesus didn't love Lazarus? Jesus loved Lazarus dearly just as He loves each of us dearly. Jesus intentionally waited two more days after learning that Lazarus was sick before He went to check on him. Why He waited is part of the plan! The delay and the timing are part of the miracle! By waiting the two extra days, Lazarus died so when Jesus arrived, He was able to do what He always intended to do – a life-saving miracle to raise Lazarus from the dead – which increased Mary, Martha, and the other's faith, which ultimately led to God's glory. If we had the chance to reschedule this miracle and change it to our timetable, we would have settled for so much less. How many times in our lives have we tried to reschedule God to fit our timetable but in His supreme goodness, He has thankfully held to the intended plan? We want what we want when we want it, but God always knows best. And just as Esther was appointed and assigned "...for such a time as this," each one of us has been given resources, purposes, opportunities, and assignments that we are to fulfill for God's kingdom and His glory. And each one of those assignments has a divine time and season that has been set before us. We can't run too far ahead of God or lag too far behind Him. When we align our timing to fall in step with God's schedule, we receive the benefit of seeing life unfold at His pace. We realize that delays are intended intervals where God purposefully waits, pauses, or lingers for us to reschedule our timetable to fit His. And the glorious miracles that are waiting for us to experience are even more amazing when we trust in His perfect timing and live life on God's timetable and not our own.

Daily Scriptures:
Monday
Habakkuk 2:3 "For still the vision awaits its appointed time; it hastens to the end—it will not lie. If it seems slow, wait for it; it will surely come; it will not delay."

What am I waiting for that I believe God has forgotten about or I see as a delay, but in reality, is Him working in His perfect timing?

Tuesday
Psalm 27:14 "Wait for the LORD; be strong, and let your heart take courage; wait for the LORD."

What does it mean to wait on the Lord?

Wednesday
1 Peter 5:6 "Humble yourselves, therefore, under the mighty hand of God so that at the proper time, he may exalt you."

How can I believe in God's "proper time?"

Thursday

Romans 8:25 "But if we hope for what we do not see, we wait for it with patience"

What does this scripture mean to me?

Friday

Lamentations 3:25-26 "The LORD is good to those who wait for him, to the soul who seeks Him. It is good that one should wait quietly for the salvation of the LORD"

How can I seek God and wait for His perfect timing in my life?

Weekly Wrap Up

Reschedule redefined:

How can I apply this to my daily life?

Week
12

Reveal

Reveal

Verb

Definition- to make something known that was once hidden

Synonyms- disclose, divulge, communicate

Two of my favorite things are sunrises and sunsets. I have to admit that since I am not much of a morning person, I have experienced many more sunsets in my life than sunrises. God is changing that reality since I have changed jobs in the past few months, and I have had the blessing to witness some glorious sunrises on the way to work. I believe that sunrises are God's way of creating a fresh start. He is not only painting a beautiful portrait for us to begin our day, but He is reminding us that His mercies are new every morning. He is revealing His ability to show Himself right before our very eyes, set the sky on fire with His glory and all we have to do is look up.

I feel that sunsets are in the same classification. They are God's way of creating hope. He is revealing to us that no matter what the circumstances of our day, at the end of the day, everything will turn out beautifully. It is by the stroke of His hand that we live and breathe and by that same hand He reveals His beauty and assurance that we can fully trust His works. These stunning gifts from God not only give us something to marvel at, but they also remind us that His plans are bigger than us and when we come to that realization, we will see the beauty in what He is doing in our lives and all around us. Again, we simply need to look up.

But the other morning when I was driving to work, I came to the place on the highway where I typically see the most amazing sunrises. I could barely see the road in front of me. The fog was so dense it seemed to cloud my vision. Cars were slowing down due to the fog, rather than taking in a blazing, colorful sunrise. But God overwhelmingly reminded me that He is in the foggy places too. Even in the spaces that I don't think are beautiful or worth oohing or awing over, He is there. Even when I don't think I can see Him, He is right in front of me and even the fog can be beautiful too.

God chooses to reveal Himself in different ways – sunrises, sunsets, a foggy morning drive to work. For Moses, it was slightly more profound. It was a normal morning for Moses, and he was on his way to work, like any other day. Moses was tending his flock according to Exodus 3 and the angel of the Lord appeared to him in a burning bush. Moses saw that the bush was on fire, but it didn't burn up. Moses didn't freak out, but he was fascinated and went to take a closer look. When God saw that Moses wasn't overwhelmed, God called to Moses from the bush. God and Moses went on to discuss God calling Moses to bring the Israelites out of Egypt (his purpose and calling in life) and Moses discussed his inability, insecurities, and doubt. We have all had these discussions with God, haven't we? And He is always right, no matter how many times we try to plead our case. Moses eventually believes the Great I AM and leads the people out from Egypt.

Several things can be learned from Moses and his burning bush encounter. God chooses how He reveals Himself to each of us. It can be a bush, a sunrise, s song, a scripture, whatever. His creation is one of the primary ways He reveals Himself. The heavens declare the glory of God, day and night (Psalm 19:1-4). He is God, and He gets to choose what and how He reveals Himself to us. The point is He is revealing Himself and we need to be aware, looking and listening.

God chooses the opportunity, time, and place. We think it will be a huge, profound burning bush moment, and for some, it just may be. But there are burning bush moments happening all around us every day. It can be sharing a cup of coffee with a hurting friend, a word of encouragement to the check-out girl at Walmart, sharing a smile with a stranger on the street or paying for the person's meal behind you in the fast-food line. We just don't know how God will use us to reveal Himself to others and become a vessel that will reveal His glory to someone who needs a touch from Him. He is moving, working, and speaking all the time. We need to be listening and obey when He calls us to act on His behalf and then we can stand back in amazement at His glorious works.

God chose to reveal Himself through a burning bush to Moses because He saw that His people were suffering. God knew that He needed to deliver them out of Egypt and wanted to use Moses to set them free. When God reveals Himself to us, He wants us to fulfill a purpose too. He wants to position us so that He can use us for His glory. It's great that He reveals Himself to us, but ultimately, it's for a purpose. Although Moses was fascinated with how the bush burned but didn't burn up, Moses was initially reluctant to obey the calling that God was giving him. We need to ask ourselves how we will respond. When God chooses to reveal Himself to us, will we be fascinated but not obedient? Will we only look for Him in the blazing sunrises and the fiery sunsets or will we also find Him in the fog? Will we hear Him on the mundane mornings that seem like any other day? Will we tell God about our inabilities, or will we believe and trust the Great I AM to use us to fulfill His purpose in the way that only He can for His ultimate power and glory?

Daily Scriptures:

Monday

Jeremiah 29:13 "You will seek Me and find Me when you seek Me with all your heart."

What does it mean for me to "seek God with all my heart"?

Tuesday

Jeremiah 33:3 "Call to Me and I will answer you and tell you great and wondrous things you to not know."

How has/does God reveal Himself to me?

Wednesday

John 1:14 "And the Word became flesh and dwelt among us, and we have seen his glory, glory as of the only Son from the Father, full of grace and truth."

How do God's creations encourage you?

Thursday

1 Corinthians 2:10 "These things God has revealed to us through the Spirit. For the Spirit searches everything, even the depths of God."

How do you respond to The Holy Spirit's call on your life to be used by Him for His glory?

Friday

Psalm 19:1 "The heavens declare the glory of God, and the sky above proclaims his handiwork."

What are some of my favorite "God creations" that remind me of His glory and power in my life?

Weekly Wrap Up

Reveal redefined:

How can I apply this to my daily life?

Week
13

Revelation

Revelation

Noun

Definition - an act of enlightening or making something known, disclosure

Synonym- unveiling, discovery, uncovering

Have you ever thought you thoroughly understood the meaning of something but when you looked at it from a completely different angle, the object or idea took on a totally different meaning? What was once clearly defined and understood takes on an entirely new reality when observed in a different light or from an alternate viewpoint. The way you perceive a concept or an idea may look one way at first, but after a good night's sleep, for instance, it may look completely different in the morning. Given a little time, a tragic event, while still devastating, may take on an entirely new reality when viewed in the rear-view mirror of our lives. The common denominator that all of these things have in common is light. When we look at circumstances, thoughts, beliefs or events in a different light, their appearances and even their meanings change, given the right light.

Or you may not understand something, someone, or a situation and you go straight to the internet as the source of your information. Google is one of my best friends. It's one of the most frequently used apps on my phone. If I have difficulty finding the answer to life's greatest challenges, I simply type my question into Google, and the answer pops right up.

This seemed to work well until I had an issue that I was struggling with on a personal level with one of my daughters, and I headed straight to Google. God stopped me in the middle of my typing, and I heard Him say, "Are you not even going to ask Me? Are you not even going to try to find the answer in My word?" That was a life-changing moment for me. He led me to Jeremiah 33:3 "Call to me and I will answer you and tell you great and unsearchable things that you do not know." Did you see it? He said unsearchable things. God promised to tell me things that not even Google knows, things that I can't even search for on the internet. Why was I surprised? Why did I not think that God knew the answers to everything, even more than what I could ask Google? Did I think it was easier to just Google it? Did I believe the internet more than I believed God? Did I trust the internet more than God? Did I like how quickly the internet would answer me, in my time? Rather than searching through my Bible and learning what His word has to say about my life, was it just simpler, more painless, and less effort to just type my question rather than opening my heart to the Lord of the universe? When God shared that He would tell me unsearchable things, I had no idea the meaning of this word. "Unsearchable" not only means something for which the answer cannot be ascertained on Google, but it also means something that cannot be fully understood or comprehended, just like the goodness and riches of Christ. We may try and search, but we will never comprehend, understand, or find the limit of Christ's riches. A few of these riches are discussed in Ephesians 1 where Paul conveys Christ's riches such as the forgiveness of sins, the wisdom of God's will, and redemption through the blood of Christ. These unsearchable truths cannot be fully understood. Rather than attempting to find information, riches, or wisdom on the internet, we should seek God and allow Him to tell us unsearchable things that we do not know.

Daily Scriptures:
Monday
Psalm 199:18 "Open my eyes, that I may behold wondrous things out of your law."

When was a time that God revealed Himself to Me in a personal way?

Tuesday
2 Timothy 3:16 "All Scripture is breathed out by God and profitable for teaching, for reproof, for correction, and for training in righteousness."

If I am being honest, do I search the scripture or the internet for answers and why?

Wednesday
2 Peter 1:21 "For no prophecy was ever produced by the will of man, but men spoke from God as they were carried along by the Holy Spirit."

What issue am I currently facing for which I need God to reveal Himself?

Thursday
John 1:18 "No one has ever seen God. But the unique One, who is himself God, is near to the Father's heart. He has revealed God to us."

How does "unsearchable" apply in my life today and what concern can I not find the answer in a Google search?

Friday
Colossians 1:15 "Christ is the visible image of the invisible God. He existed before anything was created and is supreme over all creation,"

How can I apply this truth to my life?

Weekly Wrap Up

Revelation redefined:

How can I apply this to my daily life?

Week
14

Receive

Receive

Verb

Definition – to be given, presented with, or experience

Synonyms – obtain, gain, acquire

I love to give gifts! It's one of my favorite things to do. Whether it's for someone's birthday or Christmas, or "just because" I love to find the perfect present for that person. I love to go shopping (either online or in the store) and seek out the gift that the person would absolutely love. If I have to go to several stores to find the ideal thing I know they will want, I will shop high and low to find the perfect gift. I know their size, their favorite color, their favorite scent and what they love. It's so much fun combining all of this knowledge to find the perfect present!

On the other hand, I have never been the best at receiving gifts. At Christmas, I would much rather watch others open their presents than open my own. It's not that I don't like presents, I just have never been very good at receiving them. And the gift can be amazing. The gift can be exactly what I asked for or even wanted. I am just not good at receiving. The gift does not even have to be anything physical. The present could actually be a verbal gift such as a complement or a word of encouragement. I'm still awful at receiving those kinds of gifts. Even when the gift that I am given is something that I desperately need, a compliment, a word of encouragement, a new sweater, perfume, a smile, a hug, a day off or a trip to the beach. Receiving is not one of my gifts – ha!

So, when God gives us gifts, and we aren't exactly the best at receiving, how are we supposed to respond? Because God gives great gifts! He gives them out freely, daily, without question and wanting nothing in return. He supplies all of our needs through His Son Jesus and blesses us beyond anything we can ever ask or imagine. He created Christmas, which is a time full of gifts, but we lose sight of the real gift – Jesus. So how are we to respond to the gifts He gives us when we aren't good at receiving? I mean haven't we always heard it's more blessed to give than receive? There are times in life when it is necessary to be on the receiving end because there is no giving without receiving. We just need to be grateful and gracious in the process.

I believe this is where faith plays a huge role in our lives. So many times we are striving, working, and trying to make things happen in our lives when all we have to do is ask. We are pushing, forcing and trying to rush life when we have a good Father who is waiting on us to ask. His Word says we have not because we ask not. But just because we ask, doesn't mean we will automatically get what we ask for or how we want to receive it. The giver of the gift is the one who gets to go shopping and pick out exactly what He thinks is best for us. He is the one who knows us best and knows what will fit us perfectly, what we will like and what we don't like. He knows our favorite color and our favorite foods. He knows when we need a word of encouragement, when we need a hug, a smile, a compliment or even a day of rest.

And sometimes, when we ask for something from Him, He lets us know we already have one of those in our closet. He tells us we are asking for something that He has already given us. We could be praying for guidance, wisdom, or direction and He says that we haven't taken the last step He gave us to take. He won't give us another step until we are obedient with the last step He gave us. We could be praying for the gift of forgiveness, being filled with the Holy Spirit, or His peace and God just smiles and says, girl, I gave you that a long time ago. It's been sitting in your lap for a while, waiting for you to unwrap it, put it on, and wear it every day.

So when we aren't good at receiving gifts, we need to remember that the gift giver is really the gift itself. When we receive Him, we are verbalizing our trust in Him that He always knows what is best for us. We don't have to worry about what tomorrow will hold because we know that God is already there and has placed amazing surprises along our path just for us. We know that every good and perfect gift is from above, coming down from our Father and He knows exactly what we need and when we need it. And one of the best gifts of all is today – that is why it is called the *present*. And when we stay in His gift of the present and not try to look too far ahead or live in the past, we dwell in His gifts of peace, joy, and forgiveness. And take it from someone who isn't good at receiving gifts – there is nothing better than unwrapping the perfect gift from God, that you may not even know you wanted or needed, that fits just right, at just the right time, with your name monogrammed on the front in your favorite color. And all you can say is thank you God – it's just what I wanted.

Daily Scriptures
Monday
Mark 11:24 "Therefore I tell you, whatever you ask for in prayer, believe that you have received it, and it will be yours."
Do I believe this scripture?

Tuesday
Colossians 3:23-24 "Whatever you do, work at it with all your heart, as working for the Lord, not for human masters, since you know that you will receive an inheritance from the Lord as a reward. It is the Lord Christ you are serving."
Do I seek the gift or the Gift Giver in my life?

Wednesday

Matthew 7:7 "Ask and it will be given to you; seek and you will find; knock and the door will be opened to you."

Am I asking God for something that He has already given me?

Thursday

James 1:5 "If any of you lacks wisdom, you should ask God, who gives generously to all without finding fault, and it will be given to you."

In what area of my life do I need to seek God's wisdom and direction?

Friday

2 Peter 1:3 "His divine power has given us everything we need for a godly life through our knowledge of him who called us by his own glory and goodness."

How can I see God's power at work in my life?

Weekly Wrap Up

Receive redefined:

How can I apply this to my daily life?

Week
15

Restore

Restore

Verb

Definition – return someone or something to a former condition, bring back

Synonyms – repair, fix, mend

I've always been fascinated with old homes with their antique hardwood floors, original wallpaper and historical architecture. All of these factors combine to tell a story of times gone by, people come and gone, families raised, Thanksgivings shared, tears shed, smiles exchanged, secrets shared, hugs given, and memories made. And all the while, home decorating styles have changed and paint colors have been added to the walls, new carpeting installed to cover old spills, a new layer of wallpaper to hide the old and maybe a layer or two of varnish on the hardwood floors to add a little shine. But all of these alterations never impact the primary structure of the home. Only external modifications are made to coverup and enhance the appearance of the house. Over time, these minor superficial changes accumulate to a point that a major restoration project needs to take place. The home needs to be restored to its original condition.

The same can be said about us as well. We are a lot like that beautiful antique home. We have charming architecture – some of our floors may have sunken from their original condition, but we all have stories to tell. We have weathered many storms. We have had many people come and go throughout our lives, shed tears, and made memories. Styles and fashions change, and we add a little paint here and there. We have also completed a few modifications along the way. Our layers that we use to cover up spills, messes and old pain just look a little different than wallpaper and carpet. Our layers may have different names like shame, doubt, fear, rejection, heartbreak, or pain and we have just tried to paint over those feelings. We try to bury them with in hopes that no one will ever uncover them or do a restoration project on us. We think if we just add another layer of paint, then no one will see the hurt that lies beneath the layer below.

But God wants to restore us. That has been His plan all along. That is His intention from Genesis to Revelation. He wants to bring us back to our original condition and our place with Him. Jer. 30:17 "I will restore your health and heal your wounds." That is a promise. Our health includes mental health as well. He wants to restore us and heal all of our wounds – not just physical.

And just like restoring an antique house, it won't be an overnight process. It also won't be an easy process. But as we strip away the layers of wallpaper in an old house to see the layers beneath, we relive the stories of what makes us who we are. Our past helps tell the story of who we are today and if we don't read that story from God's perspective, we will miss the point of our journey. He has been with us through it all. He continues to be with us today. As we strip away the layers of hurt, pain and fear, He reveals His purpose and shows us who we are meant to be in Him. Fully restored, back to our original condition, beautifully preserved with our interior renovated by the master engineer Himself.

Daily Scriptures
Monday

Psalm 51:12 "Restore to me the joy of your salvation and grant me a willing spirit, to sustain me."

How does God restore the joy of my salvation and sustain me with a willing spirit?

Tuesday

Psalm 23:3: NKJV "He restores my soul; He leads me in the paths of righteousness for His name's sake."

How has God's restoration in my life changed me?

Wednesday

Jeremiah 30:17 "But I will restore you to health and heal your wounds,' declares the LORD"

What do I need to remember that God has restored in my life that I may have forgotten?

Thursday

Isaiah 61:7 "Instead of your shame you will receive a double portion, and instead of disgrace you will rejoice in your inheritance. And so, you will inherit a double portion in your land, and everlasting joy will be yours."

What does this verse mean to me?

Friday

1 Peter 5:10 "And the God of all grace, who called you to his eternal glory in Christ, after you have suffered a little while, will himself restore you and make you strong, firm, and steadfast."

How can I apply this verse to my life?

Weekly Wrap Up

Restore redefined:

How can I apply this to my daily life?

Week
16

Reliance

Reliance

Noun
Definition – dependence on or trust in someone or something
Synonyms – trust, dependence

One of my favorite childhood memories is visiting my grandparents' house. As soon as we arrived, my Papaw would take me for a ride in his old green pickup truck. He and I would ride for hours on back roads all over south Tennessee and North Georgia. I had no idea where we were most of the time or where we were going, but my Papaw did. We drove for hours, rain or shine. We didn't talk much, except for a brief exchange, smile, or sweet laugh or giggle. We stopped occasionally for treats along the way – my favorites were Cola Icees and M and M's. There were mountains and valleys, twists and turns in the road but all I had to do was sit back and enjoy the view. I trusted my Papaw and relied on his navigational abilities, and I was never worried about where we were going next. I just enjoyed the ride and spending time with my Papaw.

If only I could live like that now. If only being an adult was that simple. Being an adult comes with work stress, parenting challenges, marriage struggles, financial worries, and so much more. If only I could go back to riding in that old pickup truck and have someone else drive and all I have to do is sit in the passenger seat and enjoy the scenery.

But wait. Life can be like that now. It's actually supposed to be like that now. Luke 18:16 says, "Let all the little children come to me and do not hinder them for the kingdom of God belongs to such as these." Life can be like riding in the old green pickup truck, even as an adult. I see bumper stickers all the time that say, "God is my co-pilot," but in reality, He is my pilot. He is driving the old green pickup truck and I have no idea where we are going or what lies around the next bend. There are mountains, valleys, twists and turns and He is in complete control. Some days are sunny, some cloudy, and some days have prettier scenery than others. We may talk sometimes, or He might be silent, or we might laugh and giggle along the way, but I know He is always right there beside me. We might stop for a treat every now and then, but for the most part, He is my steady, reliant driving companion who is in complete control that allows me to sit back and enjoy the ride. I simply need to give Him the wheel and have reliance in his abilities and not my own. And at the end of the day, I know He will bring me home, safe and sound.

Daily Scriptures
Monday
Proverbs 3:5-6 "Trust in the Lord with all your heart; do not depend on your own understanding. Seek His will in all you do, and he will show you which path to take"

How am I actively trusting God with all my heart and what does this look like in my daily life?

Tuesday
Isaiah 12:2 "Surely God is my salvation; I will trust and not be afraid. The Lord, the Lord himself, is my strength and my defense; he has become my salvation."

How does my trust in God keep me from being fearful?

Wednesday

Philippians 4:13 NKJV "I can do all things through Christ who strengthens me."

How does God's strength enable me to do all things in my life?

Thursday

Psalm 37:25-26 "I was young and now I am old, yet I have never seen the righteous forsaken or their children begging bread. They are always generous and lend freely; their children will be blessed."

What are some examples in my life where I have never seen the righteous shaken

Friday

Philippians 4:19 "And my God will meet all your needs according to the riches of his glory in Christ Jesus."

How can I rely on God to meet my needs?

Weekly Wrap Up

Reliance redefined:

How can I apply this to my daily life?

Week
17

Repair

Repair

Verb
Definition – to fix or restore to working order
Synonym – mend, rehabilitate, rectify

As a mom with three young daughters, going shopping was always an adventure. There were trips to the shopping mall that were more fun and relaxing and then there were the trips to the grocery store that were more task-oriented and focused. These goal-oriented shopping trips required everyone to work together to get the needed items on the shopping list. On one particular outing, I remember having three little girls under the age of six who were excited to shop with mom but did not completely grasp the goal-oriented meaning of this outing. About halfway through our adventure, the youngest was strapped in the shopping cart and was nearing the end of her time limit and patience. One of her sisters had at one point handed her a package of glow sticks and she was waving one of the sticks gladly around in the air, directing her sisters' next movements. The oldest sister grabbed the glow stick from her, which caused the youngest sister to scream loudly. I was about to yell at the oldest for taking the glow stick away when God taught me an unbelievable lesson, right there in the middle of the frozen foods section of the grocery store. The oldest sister took the glow stick and broke it so it would glow and then handed it back to her youngest sister. The youngest sister stopped crying and smiled even bigger than before seeing the bright light come from the glow stick. The oldest sister tried to explain, "I had to break it so the light would shine." If I didn't take it from you and break it, then you wouldn't see what it was really supposed to do. I stood in amazement as God used my six-year-old to speak a truth I needed to hear that day and that so many of us need to hear every day. We are broken, and that is okay. If we stayed content just being unbroken, we wouldn't be able to shine like we were intended to all along. Some of us had to lose a job, a spouse, go through a divorce, bury a parent or a child, suffer with an addiction, or with a disease of our own. It is those times of struggles and brokenness that God uses as a way for His light to shine through us. We see it as being broken but in reality, we are being repaired to be used for what He intended all along.

And what we view as broken, God has purposed to use for His glory. For example, broken soil produces crops, broken clouds allow rain to fall, broken grains produce bread and it's the broken cracks in clay pots that allow the light to shine through. All of these things that we view as broken are really repaired when placed in God's hands. The same is true when our brokenness is placed in God's hands just like the glow stick. The true reason for our creation is revealed when their brokenness is defined by God. His repair of our brokenness leads to life as it was truly intended. Difficulties, struggles, and brokenness are all around us, but they are helping us to see the reason for which we were created – being repaired according to His ways and shining His light from within our brokenness.

Daily Scriptures
Monday

Psalm 51:12 "Restore to me the joy of your salvation and uphold me with a willing spirit."

How does this scripture offer hope and encouragement to me today?

Tuesday

Isaiah 61:7 "Instead of your shame you will receive a double portion, and instead of disgrace you will rejoice in your inheritance. And so, you will inherit a double portion in your land, and everlasting joy will be yours."

What does the word "instead" in this verse mean to me and how can I apply this to my life?

Wednesday

1 John 5:4 "For everyone born of God overcomes the world. This is the victory that has overcome the world, even our faith."

How am I living today as an overcomer in Christ?

Thursday

2 Corinthians 5:17 "Therefore, if anyone is in Christ, the new creation has come: The old has gone, the new is here!"

What does it mean for me to be a new creation in Christ?

Friday

Zechariah 9:12 "Return to your fortress, you prisoners of hope; even now I announce that I will restore twice as much to you."

How is God my fortress and in what areas of my life do I need to return to Him?

Weekly Wrap Up

Repair redefined:

How can I apply this to my daily life?

Week
18

Reaction

Reaction

Noun

Definition – a reply or an action in response to a situation or event

Synonyms – response, answer, feedback

Charles Swindoll once said, "Life is 10% what happens to you and 90% how you react to it." If this statement is true, then we should have a lot of control over the circumstances of our lives. Then why don't we? If we can't always control what happens to us or the circumstances around us, according to this quote, we should at least be able to control the majority of our reactions. We realize we can't control what our boss says to us, the decisions our children make, how our spouse drives or some of his other less than competent decisions, but we do have the ability to control how we react to these actions. Although other people's choices impact us tremendously, the only thing we can regulate 100% of the time is our reactions. No one can make us feel a certain way unless we give them the power to do so. No one can make us do something or say something that we don't want to unless we allow them to have the authority over our reactions.

James 1:19 says, "Know this my beloved brothers, let every person be quick to hear, slow to speak, and slow to anger." Our reactions according to this verse are to be slow, deliberate, and not quick to anger. We have choices every day as to how we will react to people around us. We see social media posts that we can double-tap or leave a comment on. We can share, retweet, promote, post, and endorse all with the click of a button.

We can hide behind a keyboard and not even show our faces if we want to create a fake persona to say what we wouldn't want to say in person or from our own account. Our society thrives on social media with posts of hate, anger, violence, division, unsubstantiated "facts," name-calling, and belittling all in the name of media. We have a decision every day, if not every minute, about who we will follow, like, share, attach our name to, or endorse. I think we take these reactions lightly and with such little thought that not only are we so associated with our double taps and shares, but we lose sight of who are as individuals. We forget the original quote that life is 90% how we react to life, and we give that reaction away with little forethought or scrutiny. We live for other people's reactions to our posts and count desperately how many likes, shares, retweets, and comments that we receive, to the point that we forget what the actual post was about to begin with. Life. We can't live life for a post or to please our followers. We need to look up from our phones and live life. We need to realize how important our reactions are, their value and worth, and how we can react carefully and prayerfully. When our reactions align with God's word, we can rest assured that although we can't control what happens to us, we can respond in a way that promotes, endorses, and shares Jesus. When we truly live our lives for an audience of one and are concerned with His approval, we are satisfied with following the only One that matters. We know we are loved, liked, and accepted and no number of retweets, shares, or double taps can take that away. And then in turn, how we react, what we share, and the things we retweet take on new meanings as we react with purpose, rather than mindlessly. Our reactions should always be full of thought, purpose, and intention, remembering that, as stated earlier, life is determined by our reactions 90% of the time. When we live intentionally, we regain control of our lives as we regain control of our reactions and promote Jesus on our feed, share Him with our followers, and like only what is worthy of our time.

Daily Scriptures
Monday

James 1:19 "Know this, my beloved brothers: let every person be quick to hear, slow to speak, slow to anger;"

Is this verse representative of my reactions in my daily life? If not, what can I do to make the necessary adjustments?

Tuesday

Ephesians 4:2 "With all humility and gentleness, with patience, bearing with one another in love."

How am I bearing with others in love with gentleness and humility?

Wednesday

Matthew 5:39 "But I tell you, do not resist an evil person. If anyone slaps you on the right cheek, turn to them the other cheek also."

Why do I believe this scripture and how can I live this out?

Thursday

Deuteronomy 30:19 "This day I call the heavens and the earth as witnesses against you that I have set before you life and death, blessings, and curses. Now choose life, so that you and your children may live."

If our reactions have consequences, how I can choose to react positively today to my circumstances?

Friday

Proverbs 12:18 "The words of the reckless pierce like swords, but the tongue of the wise brings healing."

How are my words and reactions bringing healing to others rather than recklessly hurting them?

Reaction redefined:

How can I apply this to my daily life?

Week
19

Rely

Rely

Verb

Definition – to count on, be sure of

Synonym – depend, trust

Eagles are discussed throughout the Bible as images, analogies, and symbols. If we look at and study the eagles, they are fascinating birds. An eagle's body, life, habitat, actions, and appearance are all closely related to humans and comparisons can be drawn.

We are the eagles. Our wings represent our trust and our faith in God, and they must be spread out and extended to work. Our wings will not work if they are safely pulled in at our sides. The wind, I believe, is the Holy Spirit. Eagles fly best when an "updraft" or a strong breeze comes as eagles sit perched, waiting (Is. 40:31) for this breeze when it does come. They and we must take a leap of faith, spread their wings, and fly. Sometimes the breeze is a gentle nudge and sometimes it is a strong rush of wind, but either way, the eagle must be ready when it comes time to take flight. If the eagle stays perched safely on the limb, then she will never get to the place God intends for her to go. And while flying may sound scary at first, it is what the eagle was created to do. It is when the eagle is carried by the wind, no flapping or work required, that the eagle is in its natural state and can rest assured that the wind will take her exactly where she's supposed to go. The eagle realizes that it is not by her own power or strength (Zec. 4:6) but by His Spirit that she can soar. The eagle must learn to continually live this way of life – to wait on the wind, extend her wings, and take flight when the gush of wind arrives. If the eagle chooses to stay perched, it will die of starvation, bad weather, or a predator. If the eagle stays perched, it will never fulfill its God-given destiny and will simply watch the world pass by. But when the eagle continues to take leaps of faith and spread its faith-filled wings, the Holy Spirit-inspired wind will carry the eagle to heights she never thought possible, seeing sights the eagle could have never dreamed of and accomplishing feats the eagle could have never imagined.

Learning to live our lives like an eagle takes time, practice, and faith. When we rely on the Holy Spirit to guide us, we can fulfill our God-given destiny. Taking leaps of faith becomes a way of life and once we realize we don't need to depend on our own power or strength to fly, the next leap becomes even easier. It is then that the Holy Spirit takes us to heights we never thought possible, seeing sights we would never have been able to see sitting safely perched and soaring to destinations we never imagined.

Daily Scriptures
Monday

Isaiah 40:31 "But those who hope in the Lord will renew their strength. They will soar on wings like eagles; they will run and not grow weary; they will walk and not be faint."

What image does this scripture bring to my mind? Am I soaring like an eagle in life and if not, what do I need to adjust?

Tuesday

Isaiah 12:2 "Surely God is my salvation; I will trust and not be afraid. The Lord, the Lord himself, is my strength and my defense he has become my salvation."

How am I relying on God's strength and not my own?

Wednesday

John 14:1 "Do not let your hearts be troubled. You believe in God; believe also in me."

Is there something troubling my heart today? How can my belief in God change the struggle I am feeling in my heart?

Thursday

Isaiah 26:4 "Trust in the Lord forever, for the Lord, the Lord himself, is the Rock eternal."

How is God my eternal rock and how does that change my perspective today?

Friday

Isaiah 41:13 "For I am the Lord your God who takes hold of your right hand and says to you, do not fear; I will help you."

How does it help me today knowing God takes hold of my right hand? What do I need God's help with today?

Weekly Wrap Up

Rely redefined:

How can I apply this to my daily life?

Week
20

Require

Require

Verb

Definition – need for a particular purpose

Synonym – essential, vital, necessary

If you think about it, life has many requirements, starting early in childhood. A child cannot move to first grade without graduating from kindergarten. A student cannot go to college without the requirement of a high school diploma. A person is required to have a driver's license to drive a car. To travel to a foreign country, it is required to have a passport. There are age requirements to purchase a gun, buy alcohol, vote, or be President of the United States. Life is full of requirements, but the Bible talks about only a few.

Micah 6:8 says, "What does the Lord require of you? To act justly, to love mercy, and to walk humbly with your God." Since these requirements are biblical, let's break down what each one means in a little more depth. To act justly is also discussed in Jeremiah 22:3, "Do what is right. Rescue from the hand of the oppressor the one who has been robbed. Do no wrong or violence to the foreigner, the fatherless, the widow, and do not shed innocent blood in this place." To act justly requires us to act. The word act is an action word. If we are to do no wrong, then it should be safe to say we are to do right. We are to rescue those who need our help, and we are not to shed innocent blood. James 1:22 says we can't just be hearers of the word, but we must also be doers. Hearing God's word requires that we change our hearts, actions, and behaviors.

Next, we are required to love mercy. This may not always be easy, especially when we are offended, hurt, or wronged. To love means that we actually enjoy being merciful, so this would imply that we aren't only occasionally merciful, but that mercy is something that we love to extend to others and a response that we love to give those around us. At times we may have the right to punish someone or feel that we are justified to penalize someone for their actions, but according to this verse, we are to *love* mercy. The Bible is not saying there are no times for punishment or discipline, but according to Micah 6:8, we are to show others mercy, compassion, and forgiveness that requires some sort of sacrifice on our part instead of defaulting to anger and retribution.

And finally, the Lord requires that we walk humbly with our God. This requirement is also an action and involves applying the other two deeds to our lives. As we act justly and love mercy, we are walking humbly with God. God enables us to apply these actions to our daily walk with Him. Our walk is used to describe the path that our lives are following, and hopefully, that includes God. Walking humbly requires an abandonment of pride and arrogance and an accepting of the gifts, talents, and abilities that God has given us. It is our purpose to use all of these gifts to glorify Him. As we walk in humility, we live our lives in such a way that demonstrates a love of mercy and justice and imparts those traits to all we encounter along life's journey.

Daily Scriptures
Monday

Romans 13:10 NLT "**Love** does no wrong to others, so love fulfills the requirements of God's law."

How am I showing God's love to others in my life?

Tuesday

Romans 6:14 NLT "Sin is no longer your master, for you no longer live under the requirements of the law. Instead, you live under the freedom of God's grace."

Do I live under the freedom of God's grace in my daily life?

Wednesday

Psalm 42:1 "As the deer pants for streams of water, so my soul pants for you, my God."

Do I pant, long for, and require the Lord's presence in my life?

Thursday

John 14:15 NLT "If you love me, obey my commandments."

What does it look like in my life to love Jesus and obey His commandments?

Friday

Micah 6:8 "He has shown you, O mortal, what is good. And what does the Lord require of you? To act justly and to love mercy and to walk humbly with your God."

What are some practical ways I can act justly, love mercy, and walk humbly with God?

Weekly Wrap Up

Require redefined:

How can I apply this to my daily life?

Week
21

Reshape

Reshape

Verb

Definition – to give a new form or orientation to

Synonyms- reform, modify, alter, edit

I don't know about you, but there have been times in my life when I have felt like the mom from the movie *The Incredibles*. In the animated tale, a fictional superhero family of "incredibles" are each endowed with incredible superpowers. The mom, Elastigirl, possesses superhuman elasticity and can stretch her body parts to unbelievable proportions and then return to her natural shape and size on command. As a female, wife, mom, employee, and all the other hats that I wear daily, there are times I feel like I am stretched to great lengths only to be reshaped at the end of the day or the week for that matter. From never ending to-do lists, laundry, sports schedules, work, family, and so on, life can seem to pull us in so many different directions that by the end of the day we can feel stretched beyond our limit. Although we don't wear a cape or superhero costume, we feel as if we are carrying the world on our shoulders and our strength is measured by just how much more we can carry and handle.

If we aren't careful, we can soon realize that after all the stretching and pulling, there are times when we can't reshape ourselves. There will come a time when we won't be able to put ourselves back to our pre-stretched size, no matter how hard we try. Because if we are attempting to "do it all" in our own strength, power, and ability, we will never be able to measure up. Oh, we may be able to carry the world on our shoulders for a while and we may be able to stretch with what seems like superhero ability for a time, but eventually, we will lose our shape completely, unable to reshape ourselves. We will realize that it is God who works in us to will and to act on behalf of His good purpose (Phillipians 2:13). It is in Him we live and move and have our being (Acts 17:28). We are nothing apart from Him. We may be able to keep up the illusion for a short time that we are the ones who are doing it all, but in reality, it is all Him.

And with Jesus living in us, we are reshaped. We are His vessels, and He is constantly reshaping us. But not into superheroes that wear costumes and capes. He is making us new every day. We are being reshaped into His image and we are a work in progress. And as this process continues, we can feel stretched from time to time. It is sometimes easy to feel as if God is pulling us out of our comfort zone, but that is where growth takes place. As He reshapes us into His image, He extends our reach so that we may impact more and more people. He expands our influence in order not only to grow us but also to develop those around us. It is during this stretching that we are reshaped to look more like Jesus while He reshapes the future as well. And all this reshaping is more beneficial than any superhero could ever think about accomplishing.

Daily Scriptures
Monday

Psalm 143:6 ESV "I stretch out my hands to you; my soul thirsts for you like a parched land."

How can I stretch my hands to the Lord today?

Tuesday

Matthew 12:13 ESV "Then he said to the man, 'Stretch out your hand.' And the man stretched it out, and it was restored, healthy like the other."
How can I visualize being stretched as a positive in my life?

Wednesday

Titus 3:5 ESV "he saved us, not because of works done by us in righteousness, but according to his own mercy, by the washing of regeneration and renewal of the Holy Spirit,"
What does this scripture mean to me, and how can I apply this to my life today?

Thursday

Colossians 3:10 ESV "And have put on the new self, which is being renewed in knowledge after the image of its creator."
Am I being reshaped by putting on my new self in the image of God, my creator today?

Friday

Philippians 1:6 ESV "And I am sure of this, that he who began a good work in you will bring it to completion at the day of Jesus Christ."
How am I being molded and reshaped today by the power of the Holy Spirit?

Weekly Wrap Up

Reshape redefined:

How can I apply this to my daily life?

Week
22

Regardless

Regardless

Adverb
Definition
Synonym

As I stepped off the pier, I felt the soft, cool sand squish between my toes. My feet sank into the fluffy, white sand with each step as I wondered what this wonderful feeling was beneath my feet. The warmth of the sun baked my shoulders as I squinted to look around at all the other children playing in the sand and building sandcastles. Their laughter was contagious, and I smiled as my dad reached for my hand and we walked to find our place on the beach. As my eyes adjusted, I could see what he had been talking about for weeks – the ocean! It was beautiful! As we walked toward the ocean, the wind began to blow the salt air and I knew this was my new favorite place.

But as we got closer to the ocean, something began to happen – what was so beautiful a few minutes ago now looked ominous and scary. The waves grew bigger, and the ocean became louder and louder. My steps became slower and slower, but my dad didn't seem to realize as he continued to look ahead at our destination. I finally stopped walking and my dad turned and looked down at me. He didn't say a word as the terror was written all over my face. He could see the fear in my eyes. My dad tried to gently nudge me toward the ocean, but I wasn't budging.

He then looked at me and said, "Isn't it beautiful? You have been talking about wanting to see the ocean for weeks!" I said, "But the waves are huge!" My dad then got down on his knees and looked at the waves from my eye level. Then he understood why I was so frightened. My dad smiled at me and said, "Now I understand. It's going to be ok – I've got you, no matter what." He picked me up and carried me into the ocean so the waves wouldn't be so big and so I wouldn't be scared. We had so much fun playing in the ocean that day!

I think this is how God is. He's given me an amazing dad to love but He's an even more amazing Father – to all of us! There are so many times in our lives when we are walking on soft, fluffy sand and life seems great! We are even looking forward to something in our lives, like seeing the ocean for the first time, a big job promotion, getting married, or having children, and then when we get there and it's not what we think it's going to be. But God in His faithfulness carries us through all the ups and downs in our lives. There are other times in our lives when we feel overwhelmed, like our life is out of control, we are riding the waves of this world and we can't get our bearings, but God is there faithfully holding our hand. And then there are times like living in a global pandemic. We thought just a few weeks beforehand that everything was great, life was "normal" and all of a sudden, a giant wave came and crashed the world around us. Some people have lost their jobs or loved ones and the world seems to be out of control. In all these times – good times, uncertain times, fearful times, and sad times – God is holding us. He never lets go. He is either holding our hand and walking with us like Isaiah 41:10 says, "So do not fear, for I am with you; do not be dismayed, for I am your God. I will strengthen you and help you; I will uphold you with my righteous right hand." And other times, He picks us up and carries us. My favorite poem, "Footprints," says, "During the trials of our lives, when we look back on our lives and see only one set of footprints in the sand, it was then that HE carried us." Regardless of our circumstances – good or bad, God is always there for us.

Just like my dad could see the waves and the ocean from his higher point of view, God sees things that we cannot in our lives – from His perfect perspective. His ways are higher than our ways and His thoughts are higher than our thoughts. We don't have the privilege of seeing things from His point of view. If we did, I don't think we would be so fearful of the waves. We just might see the beauty in the unknown ocean, smell the salt air, stop, and feel the sand between our toes, and let God be God. He is there – always has been and always will be – no matter what!

Daily Scriptures
Monday
Luke 1:37 ESV "For nothing will be impossible with God."
What impossible thing am I believing God for today?

Tuesday
Isaiah 41:10 ESV "Fear not, for I am with you; be not dismayed, for I am your God; I will strengthen you, I will help you, I will uphold you with my righteous right hand."
Do I truly believe God is there for me, no matter what?

Wednesday
Proverbs 31:25 "She is clothed with strength and dignity; she can laugh at the days to come."
What am I wearing every day? Am I clothing myself in God's strength and dignity?

Thursday

Romans 8:35 NLT "Can anything ever separate us from Christ's love? Does it mean he no longer loves us if we have trouble or calamity, or are persecuted, or hungry, or destitute, or in danger, or threatened with death?"

Do I believe that anything, any situation, or any mess up that I make can separate me from God's love for me?

Friday

Romans 5:8 NLT "But God showed his great love for us by sending Christ to die for us while we were still sinners."

Do I wonder if God still loves me? Am I trying to do something that will make God love me more? Do I realize that God loves me "no matter what?"

Weekly Wrap Up

Regardless redefined:

How can I apply this to my daily life?

Week
23

Remind

Remind

Verb

Definition- cause someone to remember someone or something

Synonym – recall, remember

I'm not sure what I did before I could set reminders on my phone. (I actually forget what it was like to be able to make a quick note to remind myself to do something, set a reminder not to forget, or set an alarm to do an activity – which essentially makes my point). I still find myself putting sticky notes everywhere in addition to my phone reminders. And these reminders are coupled with dental appointment reminders, doctor appointment reminders, grocery lists, dry cleaners, and other necessary errands. But our reminders need to be appropriate, necessary, and obtainable if they are going to be successful. For instance, if I set a reminder to wake up every morning at 5:30 to go for a run I will probably run as often and as far as I would if I didn't set a reminder, which is not at all.

Determining what our priorities are and setting reminders accordingly is the first step to accomplishing new goals successfully. If we are simply setting reminders to pick up dog food, dry cleaning, or a gallon of milk on the way home from work, then maybe an app on our phone will suffice. But what if our reminders are slightly more life altering? What if we want to set reminders to pray, read God's word, or to have a quiet time with God? I'm sure there is an app for that too. But this scheduling requires that we rearrange a few priorities and set up our schedule so that God comes first. When we set our reminders to do these things – pray, read the Bible, and have a quiet time, eventually a reminder won't be needed. What happens is that God reminds us. His Holy Spirit reminds us (without an app) that we can pray anytime, any place without having to set a reminder. And during this process God also *re-minds* us. He *re-programs* our thinking during the time that we spend praying, reading, and being with Him. He *re-minds* our thoughts, taking out the old, sinful ways, and *re-filling* our minds, and making us a new creation. He *re-minds* us to think how He thinks, since His thoughts are not our thoughts and His ways are not our ways. God shows us how to align our thoughts with His – by reading His word and filling our minds with scripture.

An additional way God *re-minds* us, is through His faithfulness. As we continue to pray, read His word, and spend time with God, we will see Him show up in tremendous ways in our lives. As He demonstrates His faithfulness, we need to journal and write down God's goodness in our lives. This is a way that we can look back and remind ourselves of His devotion and reliability, especially when we are going through difficult seasons. Journaling of God's goodness can also be used to encourage others in our lives. We can remind others of His faithfulness to speak encouragement during their struggles and difficulties.

As God re-minds our minds and reminds us of His faithfulness, we are *re-programmed* to begin to think like Him. We no longer need to set reminders to spend time with Him or to pray for our friends or loved ones – it simply becomes a way of life. There is no app required to remind us to read His word because it has taken root in us. We don't need to be reminded to have a quiet time with God because we long to spend time with Him. And as He reminds our minds and hearts, our lives are forever changed and there definitely is not an app for that.

Daily Scriptures
Monday

Psalm 39:4 NLT "Remind me how brief my time on earth will be. Remind me that my days are numbered – how fleeting my life is."

What has God shown me about my time on earth and reminded me about how my life is fleeting?

Tuesday

2 Thessalonians 3:3 ESV "But the Lord is faithful. He will establish you and guard you against the evil one."

How can I remind myself of the Lord's faithfulness and his protection against the evil one in my life today?

Wednesday

Psalm 119:90 "Your faithfulness continues through all generations; you established the earth, and it endures."

How does this verse remind me that God's faithfulness endures for all time?

Thursday

2 Timothy 2:13 NLT "If we are unfaithful, he remains faithful."

How has God demonstrated His faithfulness in my life even during times of my unfaithfulness?

Friday

Nahum 1:7 "The Lord is good, a stronghold in the day of trouble; he knows those who take refuge in him."

What emotions does this verse evoke in me?

Weekly Wrap Up

Remind redefined:

How can I apply this to my daily life?

Week
24

Resolve

Resolve

Verb

Definition – to settle or find a solution, decide firmly

Synonym- decide, determine

We are faced with challenges and problems every day that we must try to resolve. These situations vary depending on the day and can include anything from an overloaded schedule, an overbearing boss, an overwhelmed child, or an overstretched budget. Even though these problems can change from day to day, the fact that we encounter daily struggles does not. And how we choose to resolve these challenges when they arise determines how successful we will be in their resolution. Our success in life is determined often times by what we decide to do ahead of time, not by waiting until a challenge arises. Let's take a look at Daniel as an example.

Daniel and his friends are taken captive in a foreign land, had their names changed and were told what they could eat and when. Daniel's life is turned upside down. He is faced with epic daily challenges and struggles. But Daniel had determined a course of action ahead of time. "But Daniel resolved not to defile himself with the royal food and wine and he asked the chief official for permission not to defile himself this way" (Daniel 1:8). Daniel determined the *what* before he knew the *how*. He realized that his success in life is determined by what he decided to do ahead of time, not by waiting for the challenge to appear. We can have this same resolve in our lives today, but we must prepare ahead of time like Daniel. We must realize that challenges will come, and struggles will arise, and we must determine ahead of time what we believe in order to be able to decide what we will do.

As we follow Daniel and his friends, we see that they engaged their culture without compromising their beliefs. They listened in an attempt to understand other's hearts, but Daniel and his friends did not compromise their convictions. We are called to live in this world but not be of this world. Just like Daniel and his friends, we are to live wisely among non-believers making the most of every opportunity (Colossians 4:5). This enables us to impact their lives, using wisdom in our interactions and showing grace, love, and mercy. We should impact their lives more than we allow them to impact our lives and we should seize every opportunity that God gives us. "Daniel went to the king and asked for time that he might interpret the dream for him" (Daniel 2:16). God opens doors for us. We must pray for those opportunities and seize them when they come. God will typically use the gifts He has placed within us when He opens the doors; we walk through for Him. God has gifted each one of us uniquely and will utilize those gifts when we seize opportunities to use them for His glory.

Finally, we can resolve our problems when we resolve to leave the results to God. When our resolve or strong determination is that we trust God with our outcomes, we can live without fear of the future. Daniel and his friends, Shadrach, Meshach, and Abednego, lived in obedience to God. They did not need to defend themselves before King Nebuchadnezzar when he required that they bow to and worship his golden idol rather than the Lord God Almighty. When Nebuchadnezzar threw them into the fiery furnace for their obedience to God, they resolved to trust God with their outcome. They resolved to leave the results in God's hands. They resolved their problems by trusting in the One who gets into the furnace with us, protects us from the flames of difficulties, and walks with us through heartache. When we live in obedience to God and resolve to trust Him with our future, we stand boldly on His word and promises to always be with us in the fire. We live fearlessly knowing that He resolves our problems and whatever comes our way, He will never leave us. When we honor God, He will honor us. We simply need to resolve to leave the results to Him and let Him resolve our problems the way that He sees best.

Daily Scriptures
Monday
Colossians 1:11 "May you be strengthened with all power according to his glorious might so that you may have great endurance and patience."
How does this scripture enable me to resolve to leave the results of my life to God?

Tuesday
1 Peter 5: 6 "Humble yourselves, therefore, under God's mighty hand, that he may lift you up in due time."
If I live my life according to this verse, what will change and how might life look differently?

Wednesday
Ephesians 4:32 NLT "Be kind and compassionate to one another, forgiving each other, just as God through Christ has forgiven you."
How can I resolve to forgive others in my life, as Christ has forgiven me?

Thursday
Psalm 101:2 NLT "I will be careful to lead a blameless life – when will you come to help me? I will lead a life of integrity in my own home?"

How can I resolve to live a life of integrity, especially in my own home?

Friday
2 Thessalonians 1:11 "With this in mind, we constantly pray for you, that our God may make you worthy of his calling, and that by his power he may bring to fruition your every desire for goodness and your every deed prompted by faith."

What does this verse mean to me and how does "resolve" apply to this verse?

Weekly Wrap Up

Resolve redefined:

How can I apply this to my daily life?

Week
25

Remain

Remain

Verb

Definition – continue to stay in a place for a significant amount of time
Synonym – stay, wait, abide

Our society is a people filled with a "go" mentality. We love to be on-the-go. We fill our calendars with events, ballgames, dinners, parties, weddings, practices, appointments, and many other occasions that we may not even want to attend. We love to be busy and feel as if a filled calendar symbolizes a filled life. When the COVID-19 pandemic hit in the spring of 2020, our lives changed, and we were forced to limit our schedules and our calendars. We all remained in our homes and life came to a standstill all over the world. As we remained in our homes and our way of life radically altered, people began to reexamine their priorities, shift their way of thinking, and modify their schedules. Working from home, ordering groceries from home, teaching our children from home, and even attending church from our living rooms became a new way of life. We learned how to remain in our homes but were we really remaining? God's definition of remaining varies from our definition.

John 15 says, "Remain in me, and I will remain in you. No branch can bear fruit by itself; it must remain in the vine. Neither can you bear fruit unless you remain in me. I am the vine; you are the branches. If a man remains in me and I in him, he will bear much fruit; apart from me you and do nothing. If anyone does not remain in me, he is like a branch that is thrown away and withers; such branches are picked up, thrown in the fire, and burned. If you remain in me and my words remain in you, ask whatever you wish, and it will be given you" (John 15:4-7). From these verses we can see that remaining is an action verb and not merely a passive way of living. Remaining is not just sitting at home passively waiting for life to happen while a worldwide pandemic is occurring all around us. Remaining is actively doing according to John. Remaining requires that we vigorously live our lives in Christ. We must actively be a participant in the production of fruit in our lives. During the global pandemic, there were countless stories of people who started new businesses, created new products, and developed innovative ways of solving problems. There were stories of families growing closer together and closer to God. There were reports of people overcoming challenges and impossible struggles and faced insurmountable odds all while remaining at home. Remaining requires action.

 Remaining also requires faith. Matthew 14 discusses the account of Jesus walking on water and Peter stepping out of the boat and walking to Him. I have prayed on several occasions to have great faith like to Peter to have "water-walking faith" and to live my life unafraid like Peter. But I also believe there are times that it requires great faith to live like the other disciples who remained in the boat. There are times in our lives when we are in a storm and we need the faith to remain. There are times it requires more faith to remain. Our marriage may be struggling and rather than jump ship, it requires more faith to remain and stay faithful in the marriage. Our child may be wavering off course and not be living the life we intended for them. But rather than jump ship, we remain faithful and pray for them, not wavering in our faith. Remaining requires the action of staying grateful, praying, and praising God in the storm. Big steps of faith do not always require big steps. Those steps can be steps that simply prove our ability to remain in tough times through difficult situations. And as we remain in faith, God remains faithful to us. He continues to prove His faithfulness over and over to us and we realize that we can do nothing apart from Him but we, like the branch discussed in John 15, can bear much fruit when we remain in Him.

As we slowly begin to reemerge from the global pandemic and start to fill our calendars again, I pray we never forget what it feels like to remain. And not just remaining in our homes, but that we have a new sense of remaining in God. I hope we apply John 15 to our daily lives and remain a people who stay faithful to His word, to prayer, to gratitude and to worship no matter where we remain, whether in our homes or not.

Daily Scriptures
Monday
1 Corinthians 13:13 "And now these three remain: faith, hope, and love. But the greatest of these is love."
Why do I believe the greatest of these three attributes is love?

Tuesday
Psalm 27: 13 "I remain confident of this: I will see the goodness of the Lord in the land of the living."
How can I remain confident that I will see God's goodness today and every day?

Wednesday
John 15:5 "I am the vine; you are the branches. If you remain in me and I in you, you will bear much fruit; apart from me you can do nothing."
How can I remain in Jesus according to John 15?

Thursday

Esther 4:14 "For if you remain silent at this time, relief and deliverance for the Jews will arise from another place, but you and your father's family will perish. And who knows but that have come to your royal position for such a time as this?"

What could have been the consequences for Esther and her family if she remained silent? What is a situation currently or in your past that has dire consequences if you remain silent?

Friday

James 1:12 ESV "Blessed is the man who remains steadfast under trial, for when he has stood the test he will receive the crown of life, which God has promised to those who love him."

What are some specific ways I can remain steadfast under trial or challenging circumstances in my life?

Weekly Wrap Up

Remain redefined:

How can I apply this to my daily life?

Week
26

Relax

Relax

Verb

Definition – loosen up, sit back, recline

Synonyms – calm, unwind, soften

Stress is all around us. We can't escape it. We all define stress in different ways. What may be extremely stressful for me may not be stressful for you and vice versa. You may find a situation incredibly stressful, and I may not think anything about it. However, there are a few universal events or occurrences that everyone finds stressful. Death of a family member, friend, or loved one, divorce, job loss, health crisis, and financial strain are examples of universal stressors that most people find incredibly stressful. These events tend to impact all of us negatively and can lead to anxiety, worry, and fear if not handled in a Christ-centered way. But there are also everyday stressors that we encounter that can lead to these same emotions. Waiting, feeling like life is out of our control, wondering if we are enough, and doubts about our future are just a few examples that can create feelings of stress in our lives. I think these feelings can be universal to an extent as well. My doubts about the future may not be the same as yours, but the stress is still the same. And I believe these feelings were experienced by those living in biblical times as well. Let's look at an example.

In Mark 6, Jesus' miracle of feeding the 5,000 is described. This is a well-known miracle and has been discussed at length over the years. But as someone who is a pre-planner and a little more than OCD, this miracle has always stressed me out. Jesus is preaching, ministering to, and loving on a huge crowd of people. It is getting late in the day. The planner in me wonders why someone didn't start thinking about dinner. But then that would have removed the opportunity for the miracle. So, the stress begins, or so I think. The people begin to get hungry and there is not enough food for 5000 people. Jesus finds out about the need and that there is not enough food after it is too late to do anything about it. The disciples determined that it was too late to do anything about it and were stressed, but Jesus just wanted to know what they actually had to work with. What did they have that He could use? He didn't want to know what they didn't have. Jesus wanted the disciples to know that what they had was enough. He didn't need for the disciples to argue and tell Him that the five loaves of bread and two fish were not enough. Jesus knew that anything they had plus Him equals enough. It is the same with our lives. We feel like we are not enough. How many times have you argued with Him that you aren't enough? We create undue stress by looking at what is in our hands and telling Jesus that there is no way that is going to be enough. There is no possible way that He can use what we have in our hands to feed anyone. We feel that we have so little, and it wouldn't be possible for Him to use what we have. We do not even realize that whatever we have, plus Jesus, always equals enough. Whatever we have in our hands, He placed there in the first place, so He has the ability to multiply it to meet any need we have. We simply need to relax our hands, give Him our five loaves and two fish, and let Him multiply them to feed those around us. When we relax our hands and give Jesus what we are holding, two things happen. First, when we give Him what we are holding, He can multiply it, making it possible to feed those around us and making us enough in the process. Second, it opens our hands to receive more from Him than if we hold onto what we are holding with clenched fists. We can save ourselves undue stress if we relax our hands, give Jesus what we are holding, and allow Him to use us to bless and feed those around us. We are always enough when we give Jesus all we have. It only becomes enough when we give it to Him. We relax and let Him do the miracle, which relieves the stress of today. As we daily give Him what is in our hands, whether that is struggles, challenges, joy, peace, or adversity, He forms it in such a way that it can be used to feed others. If we hold onto these things, in our own strength it is never enough. But in a relaxed hand, with a relaxed mind and heart, God transforms these things in such a way that others can be fed, lives are altered, and baskets are overflowing with more than enough for today.

Daily Scriptures
Monday

Exodus 33:14 "My presence will go with you, and I Will give you rest."
How does this verse help me cope with stress and to relax?

Tuesday

Matthew 11:28 ESV "Come to me, all who labor and are heavy laden and I will give you rest."
How can I apply this verse in my life today?

Wednesday

Psalm 23:1 ESV "The Lord is my shepherd; I shall not want. He makes me lie down in green pastures. He leads me beside still waters."
What does it mean to me today that the Lord is my shepherd, and He makes me relax, and lie down in green pastures? What does that look like in my life today?

Thursday

Psalm 91:1-2 ESV "He who dwells in the shelter of the Most High will abide in the shadow of the Almighty. I will say to the Lord 'My refuge and my fortress, my God, in whom I trust."

Am I truly dwelling in the shelter of God and how does this allow me to rest in His shadow as I go through my day?

Friday

Psalm 4:8 ESV "In peace, I will both lie down and sleep; for you alone, O Lord, make me dwell in safety."

How will this verse impact me as I go to bed tonight?

Weekly Wrap Up

Relax redefined:

How can I apply this to my daily life?

Week
27

Refuse

Refuse

Verb
Definition- turn away and not accept
Synonyms- renounce, decline, deny

Life is full of absolutes, at least for most people. I am one of those people. I absolutely will not go late into a movie. I absolutely refuse to go skydiving or hang gliding and, at this point in my life, I won't even ride most roller coasters or climb anything higher than my front porch. But what about other absolutes that I have grown a voice to refuse in my life? I refuse to justify going to bed early, explain why I'm not wearing make-up when I don't feel like it, place someone's else opinion above mine when my prayers and intuition validate my instinct, define success monetarily, apologize for my faith, or defend for my love for my family and friends. I refuse to start my day without smiling, praying, and thanking God or without a plan. There are a few more "absolutes" in my life, but most important is that I absolutely refuse to let go of God's hand and His direction in my life.

Deuteronomy 30 is a chapter in the Bible chocked full of insight from God. His promises of mercy are discussed but it's the last few verses of this chapter I want to highlight. In verses 15-20, Moses lays out choices before the Israelites before they enter the Promised Land. He lays before them good and evil, describing the consequences of what will happen as a result of their choices. If they choose to turn away from God and worship other gods, then death and destruction will follow; they will be cursed and die. But if they choose life, God's blessings will follow; He will lengthen their days. Moses gives specific instructions as to how to choose God and to follow Him. Deuteronomy 30:20, in short, says to Love God, obey His voice, and refuse to let go—three simple instructions that we can all apply to our lives every day.

Instructions to love God are found throughout the Bible. Mark 12:30 reminds us that we are to love the Lord with all our heart and soul, mind, and with all our strength. That is pretty much everything we have. If we are focusing on loving God with all that we have, then we have surrendered our lives to Him, are following Him every day, spending time with Him in prayer, and serving Him and others in His name. The second of Moses' instructions naturally follows in our lives.

When we spend time with God, we will "hear" gentle nudges of the Holy Spirit and a stillness of God that resonates with our spirit. He speaks, directs, and leads everyone in different ways. He leads us through His word, through the Godly wisdom of other believers, through music and worship and however else He chooses to lead us. How He leads me will not be the same as how He leads you, but the leading is still the same. And how He may have spoken last time may not be the same way He speaks to us this time. The point is that we need to obey His leading. Moses' second instruction to the Israelites is to obey His voice. That voice, according to Psalm 29, is over the waters, thunders, is powerful, majestic, and breaks trees. But that voice also, according to I Kings 19, was not in the fire or an earthquake but was the sound of a gentle blowing. God is God and He spoke this earth, man, and animals into existence, so He can choose to speak however He chooses. Our part is to obey what He says to us and to not let go.

Refusing to let go is a rare trait these days. Divorce rates are sky high, even within the church. We leave jobs just because someone offended us, or we don't like who we work with, or the work may get a little challenging. Holding on when things get tough is not an easy request and Moses knew what he was asking of the Israelites. These people had been wandering for forty years in the wilderness under his leadership and he was asking them to not let go. Moses knew he was nearing the end of his life, and he was imparting his deathbed wisdom. He wanted them to enter the Promised Land blessed. Refusing to let go was a rare trait, even in Moses' day, and he wanted the Israelites to cling to God, not only for themselves, but for their descendants as well. Likewise, this truth needs to be translated to our lives today. Refusing to let go, as rare as it is today, needs to be foundational in our lives. When things get tough, we need to refuse to let go of God. We need to cling to Him just as Moses pleaded with the Israelites. And not only for our sake, but for our family's sake as well. When our marriage is struggling, then we need to grasp even tighter to God's word and refuse to let go. He promises to never let go of us. Isaiah 41:10 says, "Fear not, for I am with you, be not dismayed, for I am your God; I will strengthen you, I will help you, I will uphold you with my righteous right hand." He holds our hand. We simply need to refuse to let go of His. We need to listen to the wise words of Moses and have the rare trait of holding on. If we refuse to let go and be a people that love God and obey His voice in our lives, then when the choices are placed in front of life and death or blessings and curse, then we should obtain a long, fruitful, good life like Moses described to the Israelites. So, if set before you today, life and death, blessing and curse, holding on or letting go, which do you choose?

Daily Scriptures
Monday
Proverbs 8:33 ASV "Hear instruction and be wise. Don't refuse it."
Am I hearing and obeying God's direction in my life?

Tuesday

Job 6:7 "I refuse to touch it; such food makes me ill."
What are some absolutes in my life that I refuse?

Wednesday

1 Timothy 4:7 "Have nothing to do with godless myths and old wives' tales; rather, train yourself to be godly."
Are there any old ideas, customs, or myths I believe that need to checked and surrendered so I can train myself to be godly?

Thursday

2 Timothy 2:23 "Don't have anything to do with foolish and stupid arguments, because you know they produce quarrels."
How can I refuse to engage in stupid arguments and needless quarrels?

Friday

Matthew 10:33 "But whoever disowns me before others, I will disown before my Father in heaven."
How can I refuse to deny Jesus in my life as I interact with others today?

Weekly Wrap Up

Refuse redefined:

How can I apply this to my daily life?

Week
28

Regrow

Regrow

Verb
Definition – make something new again
Synonyms – develop, produce, invigorate

I love fruit, but only certain kinds of fruit. Pineapples, bananas, apples, oranges, and grapes are just a few of my favorites. But I am always disappointed when I want to buy strawberries in the grocery store, and they aren't in season. When I want strawberries, grapes will not suffice. So, this got me thinking. Why do some fruits grow better in some seasons than others? Why are some fruits seasonal and some fruits available all year round?

When I researched the variables in fruit growth, many factors come into play. Sunlight, pollinators, hydration, day length and place of growth – tree, ground, or bush for example. When you think of running to the store to pick up a watermelon or an avocado (yes that's a fruit), there is a lot that goes into how they are developed and raised.

Certain fruits require more sunlight than others. They need higher temperatures, and they adapt to changes in sunlight, but these fruits tend to thrive when there is more sunlight and heat. These fruits include bananas, squash, and melons. Then some fruits thrive year-round and can survive regardless of changes in the weather. Apples, peaches, and the incredibly famous grapefruit will flourish year-round. I believe we are a lot like the seasonal fruits that require more sunlight in order to thrive. We need the Son, Jesus, in order to flourish. We need His light guiding us in order to grow and develop into what we are supposed to be in life. We are called to produce fruit and we need His light in order to do that. If we don't have that light, then we can't produce fruit, no matter how hard we try. Producing fruit in certain seasons of our lives requires constant light because it is impossible to grow fruit in the dark. It just won't happen. But just as these fruits thrive seasonally, we are called to be year-round producers and thrive in conditions that may not be optimal. We will produce fruit that we may not have expected. We simply need to stay close to the light.

Fruit also needs pollinators for production. Pollinators are critical for fruit production and include honeybees, bumble bees, butterflies, other insects or even the wind. Pollination is needed to distribute the pollen for growth and helps to produce the fruit seeds in the trees and plants. What may look like a pest or predator is actually helpful in fruit production. Just like in life, what we may view as something detrimental, scary, or something that stings us or hurts, can actually be used to produce fruit in our lives. We can see a bumble bee of an event in our lives and feel the sting of that experience, but if we allow God to use it in His way, the pain of the sting will actually help to produce fruit. It will pollinate our life in such a way that good fruit is ultimately produced. Beautiful experiences like butterflies can be used to produce fruit in our lives too. God places wonderful people in our lives who look like exquisite butterflies to pour into us and to aid in our fruit production. God uses the Wind, or the Holy Spirit, to produce fruit in our lives too. A gentle breeze of the Holy Spirit can be extremely beneficial in fruit production. All of these things are necessary in developing, growing, and producing fruit in our lives.

Hydration is a key component to fruit production. Fruits need water to grow. But we as humans need water to grow too. Jesus refers to Himself as the source of living water and whoever drinks the water He gives will never thirst again. (John 4:14) As we drink of this water, we will grow and produce God's fruit in our lives. And this is interesting because as we grow and produce fruit, most fruits are composed primarily of water. Cucumbers are 95% water, lettuce is 96% water, and watermelons are 92% water. When we produce the fruit that God calls us to produce—love, joy, peace, patience, kindness, goodness, faithfulness, gentleness, and self-control—then these fruits are fully hydrated as well. These spiritual fruits are full of His hydration that He poured into us and enabled us to produce.

Some fruits are grown closer to the equator and require a longer day. Some fruits do not require a long day to develop and grow. Some fruits continue to ripen even after they have been picked. Apricots, bananas, cantaloupe, kiwi, and pears continue to ripen even after they have been harvested. These fruits continue to grow even when resting and one would think they are finished developing. We all need rest, but some of us need a little more than others, and that is okay. During times of rest, we grow. We need rest in order to grow, replenish, and prepare for still more progress. In times when we think we are way past our harvest point or overly ripe, God reminds us that we still have some growing to do or that we still need to develop in certain areas. Alternatively, we may think we can't be used because we have been plucked for too long, we are too old, or we are past our prime, but God reminds us that fruit continues to ripen after being picked . Our maturity doesn't depend on our timetable, but on God's schedule. His harvest is what matters, and our fruit production is in His hands.

Finally, where the fruit is grown determines the type of fruit that is produced. Some fruit is grown on trees, some on the ground, and some fruit is grown on bushes. Fruits like apples, bananas, oranges, and pears grow on trees while other fruits grow on bushes like strawberries, peppers, tomatoes, and pineapples. And then there are fruits that grow on the ground while they grow like watermelon, lettuce and cantaloupe. The various means in which fruits grow is determined by God. He knows how the fruit will best flourish. He knows that strawberries aren't intended to grow on trees and apples were never intended to grow on the ground. The same is true for you and me. God knows the conditions in which we flourish best and the manner in which we are intended to grow. He knows that if we are a strawberry, we aren't supposed to try to grow like a banana. This sounds like an absurd example, but there are many of us trying to live our lives as something we were never intended to be, and we are attempting to produce fruit that was never ours to produce. There some of us trying to grow apples from watermelon seeds. God has placed seeds in each one of us. His seeds. Seeds that He didn't place in anyone else. These seeds are meant to produce an expected result and it isn't really our say what kind of fruit we are. God made us how we are and the seeds that are in us will bear the fruit that we are called to bear. It's our job to stay close to the Son, use the pollinators, both good and bad, in our lives, drink in His hydration, create space to rest, stay on His timetable and schedule, and develop into the fruit that God intended for us to become, not someone or something we are not called to be. It's during these processes that fruit production takes place, in every season of our lives. Everything we experience aids in the development of becoming who God has called us to be. By being true to your authentic calling, your fruit not only is beneficial to you, but it helps everyone around you as well.

Daily Scriptures
Monday

2 Peter 3:18 "But grow in the grace and knowledge of our Lord and Savior Jesus Christ. To Him be the glory both now and forever. Amen!"

How am I actively growing in the grace and knowledge of Jesus?

Tuesday

1 Thessalonians 3:12 "May the Lord make your love increase and overflow for each other and for everyone else, just as ours does for you."
How is my love for others growing through my faith in Jesus?

Wednesday

Psalm 51:12 ESV "Restore to me the joy of your salvation and uphold me with a willing spirit."
How does my salvation bring me joy today?

Thursday

1 Corinthians 11:1 ESV "Be imitators of me, as I am of Christ."
How am I regrowing to be an imitator of Christ after challenges in my life?

Friday

James 1:2 ESV "Count it all joy, my brothers, when you meet trials of various kinds,"
How can I view trials with joy and grow in my relationship with Jesus?

Weekly Wrap Up

Regrow redefined:

How can I apply this to my daily life?

Week
29

Repetition

Repetition

Noun

Definition – the act of continuing an activity without interruption
Synonyms – duplication, iteration, repeat

I have several allergies and I believe one of them is I am allergic to exercise. I have a reaction every time I work out. I get sore, my body hurts, and I have difficulty moving the next day after working out. I'm pretty sure my body has an aversion to exercise. However, the more often I work out, the less the adverse reaction is on the following day. The more often I repeat the exercises, the less I have the unpleasant effects. And I realize the exercises are beneficial to me, I just need the diligence and determination to adhere to the repetitions in my lifestyle so hopefully the allergic reaction will eventually subside. Using these muscles in new ways to build strength is what the exercise is intended for and helps to make me stronger. Although there is pain after the repetitions, the end result is eventually newfound power and strength. Stretching these muscles to new lengths will eventually cause them to grow, increase their flexibility and make them healthier than they were prior to stretching. Exercising and stretching will also help in preventing future injuries. Realizing these truths and incorporating them into our daily routine is the way to not only build strength, but increase flexibility in our bodies.

However, I find myself just going through the motions some days. I don't know about you, but for me, there are some days that seem to turn into weeks; I don't seem to know where the time has gone. I feel like the ball in a pinball machine that just bounces from one event to another or from one place to another. Going through the motions, showing up just to be there, and doing the same thing over and over every day can become boringly repetitious. Just repeating the same day with the same schedule over and over, while safe and secure, can become monotonous. Exercise is the last thing on my mind and the last thing I incorporate into my schedule. Allowing the same events to fill my schedule and my time do not require planning, forethought, or uncertainty. If we spend our days within our comfort zone, then we are safe and secure within our limits. We know what to expect next. We know who we will see each day, where we will spend our day, and exactly what our schedule will be so that there is no room for unexpected outcomes. If we do not deviate from our routines, then there will not be anything unique about our lives.

I believe this kind of life has the potential to schedule God right out of it. We aren't living life intentionally. We need to live on purpose. God has called us for a purpose. He created us for a purpose, and we need to seek that out and live according to the purpose and plans that He has for our lives. "Whatever we eat, drink, or whatever we do, do it all for the glory of God" (1 Corinthians 10:31). *Whatever* includes everything. Everything we do we need to do to give God glory. We need to commit to living for Him. This type of lifestyle will stretch us. It will draw us out of our comfort zones. This type of lifestyle will require that we exercise a few muscles that we haven't used in a while. We may need to stretch a few muscles that have been sedentary. We will need to start walking differently than we have in the past. Some of us may need to start walking altogether. We will need to breathe a little deeper as we move in ways that we haven't moved before. And this new lifestyle will need to become repetitious in order to become a habit. We will need to become disciplined to our new lifestyle and exercise these new habits. When we remember that whatever we do, we work for God with all our hearts and not for man (Colossians 3:23). Even our jobs will develop a new purpose when we work according to this mindset. As with working out and exercising, repetitions are called "reps" for short. When we lift weights or do multiple sets of an exercise, it is called a rep. Every time we take a step out of our comfort zone, climb over a new challenge, or balance a fresh set of adversities, we are creating new levels of endurance. When we stretch our faith muscles, we are increasing our flexibility for future oppositions. An increase in flexibility aids in prevention of future injury. Being flexible allows us to face challenges and adversities with strength and endurance. Our faith in God is ultimately what gives us our strength and power. Through the repetition of trusting Him over and over, we build our faith muscles to endure what lies ahead. When we begin each day in surrender to His will and say "Here I am Lord, send me. Is there anything new you have for me today?" then He provides the strength and ability for us to face the day. When this becomes our daily repetition, we will no longer be a pinball bouncing from one place to another. We will live intentionally, in His freedom, not just going through the motions, but living life to the fullest, becoming stronger through daily repetitions of powerful surrender.

Daily Scriptures
Monday

Matthew 6:7 ESV "And when you pray, do not heap up empty phrases as the Gentiles do, for they think that they will be heard for their many words."

When I consider my prayer life, am I more concerned about repeating what I think I am supposed to say, or what I think God wants to hear, or I am talking to God from my fully transparent heart?

Tuesday

Matthew 15:8 "These people honor me with their lips, but their hearts are far from me."

Am I just going through the motions during times of worship or is my heart truly devoted to the Lord and not just on outward expressions?

Wednesday

Matthew 22:37 "Jesus replied: "'Love the Lord your God with all your heart and with all your soul and with all your mind."

Do I truly love the Lord with all these parts of me – my heart, soul and mind?

Thursday

Hosea 6:6 ESV "For I desire mercy, not sacrifice, an acknowledgement of God rather than burnt offerings."

Am I simply marking off boxes in my Christian activity, such as occasionally reading my Bible, going to church on Sundays, and giving money from time to time, or am I experiencing a vibrant, authentic relationship with Jesus?

Friday

John 10:10 ESV "The thief comes only to steal and kill and destroy. I came that they may have life and have it abundantly."

Am I living the abundant life Jesus promises in which I know Him and am known by Him as I truly follow His ways in my daily life?

Weekly Wrap Up

Repetition redefined:

How can I apply this to my daily life?

Week
30

Reach

Reach

Verb

Definition – to get to, arrive at, to enter or impact

Synonyms- accomplish, attain, achieve

I love reminiscing and looking at old photos. I made scrapbooks for my daughters when they were young and documented every stage of their lives including family vacations, school milestones, and athletic mementos. I love to look back over their childhoods and remember sweet days gone by. Sadly, there are times when I look at these photos and think to myself, I wish I could back to those days. I wish I had those precious little girls still living at home, ambling down the stairs in the mornings, fighting over each other's clothes, and staying up way too late. I want to reach back into those pages of the scrapbook and grab that young version of myself and tell her so many things. I want to reach back to those days gone by and try to relive the past and maybe have a few do-overs. Maybe with the knowledge that I have today, I might not mess up as much as I think I did back then. Maybe if I could reach back, I could encourage that young mom who had no idea what she was doing with three precious gifts from God; I could tell her to enjoy every second because it goes by way too fast. But then I need to realize we are never intended to live our lives in the past. Scrapbooks, as wonderful as they are, are simply meant as sweet memories of days that have gone by and no matter how hard we try, we can't reach back. We were never meant to reach back, only glance back and smile. Just like a car has a huge windshield and a small rearview mirror. The windshield is for viewing where we are headed, and the rearview mirror is for where we have been. We are meant to give the same proportionate priority to our lives. We are to only look back in the rearview mirror occasionally to see where we have been, but our focus should always be where we are headed.

Paul discusses this forward-thinking process on Philippians 3:13-14 "Brothers and sisters I do not consider myself yet to have taken hold of it. But one thing I do: Forgetting what is behind and straining toward what is ahead. I press on toward the goal to win the prize for which God has called me heavenward in Christ Jesus." Our reach, according to Paul, should always be forward and not back. He says we should always be striving toward our goal, which is looking toward heaven. This isn't our home. We are just passing through. And although we are called to make a difference in the lives we encounter while we are here on earth, our ultimate goal is heaven. Oswald Chambers said, "A man's reach should exceed his grasp." Heaven, on our own, is beyond our grasp. We should strive to live faith-filled lives that far exceed our grasp. In doing so, we attempt prayerful feats, showcasing the power and faithfulness of God so that it's clear He alone deserves the honor and glory. When we reach beyond our grasp, we live in a way that allows room for the Holy Spirit to move, act and show up in powerful ways. We should never be content with our current level of spiritual growth or maturity but always reach for and strive to new levels of intimacy with God. This is one area of our lives where contentment and satisfaction should be challenged. We should continually reach for more growth through serving Him, discipleship, prayer, worship—whatever it is that God is calling you to do for Him.

God often places promises within our reach but not in our hands. His promises will require faith, trust, and obedience on our part as we reach to obtain them. In Exodus 6, God is promising the Israelites He will deliver them from slavery in Egypt. This promise was not within their grasp, but nonetheless it was within their reach because God had promised it. This promise required faith, trust, and obedience on their part. We can learn from this portion of scripture that even though something promised is not placed in our hands, God's promises are always within our reach. Exodus 6:6 says, "I will free you from being slaves to them and I will redeem you with an outstretched arm." Just as God reaches out an outstretched arm, we must reach out as well to grasp ahold of Him. God's outstretched arm symbolizes power and strength. We are never beyond His reach. We never stray so far that He cannot reach us. His outstretched arm can always grasp and reach us. Although God places promises in our reach but not in our hands, we must stretch our hands out in order to grasp and obtain them. We can trust that His promises remain true today. His word never fails us and He will never leave or forsake us. But we must reach out in faith in order to grasp everything that God has for us.

And even though we can look back through old scrapbooks and remember God's faithfulness, we are not called to stay focused on the past. We can't get stuck in the "glory days" or wish we could go back in time. Don't become fixated on old hurts, regrets, pains or condemnation. We aren't called to relive our past – whether good or bad. We are simply to glance in the rearview mirror of our lives and build faith on what God has done for us. We are to trust the promises that God has placed within our reach and with His help, strive to trust and obey His word in order to accomplish all that He has for us today. With our sights on heaven, we can reach our final destination knowing His promises were true and real everyday of our lives.

Daily Scriptures
Monday
Philippians 3:14 ESV "...press on toward the goal for the prize of the upward call of God in Christ Jesus."

Am I reaching for God's call on my life as my primary life's goal?

Tuesday
Mark 16:15 ESV "And he said to them, "Go into all the world and proclaim the gospel to the whole creation."

Even if I am not physically going on a global mission trip, how am I reaching the nations for the gospel of Jesus?

Wednesday
Psalm 139:7 "Where can I go from your Spirit? Where can I flee from your presence?"

Do I understand that even though I may be fighting old habits, overwhelmed with life's challenges, or struggling with past decisions, I am never out of God's reach? How can I know this truth and apply this reality in my life today?

Thursday
Romans 15:7 "Accept one another, then, just as Christ accepted you, in order to bring praise to God."

Who can I reach out to today and share God's love with?

Friday
Psalm 18:6 ESV "In my distress I called upon the Lord; to my God I cried for help. From his temple he heard my voice, and my cry to him reached his ears."

When is a time that I have cried out to God, and He has reached down and answered my prayers? How can this reminder encourage me today?

Weekly Wrap Up

Reach redefined:

How can I apply this to my daily life?

Week
31

Re-examine

Re-examine

Verb

Definition – to take another careful look

Synonym – reconsider, review

There is nothing like a good crime show on television. I love all kinds of crime dramas, especially the television shows in which a crime is committed and then all the clues need to be collected, calculated, and examined in order to solve the mystery. One of my favorite shows is *CSI: Crime Scene Investigation*. In this particular television drama, the crimes are solved by a highly trained team that collects specimens and clues, examines these elements of a crime scene, and pieces together evidence to decipher the mystery. The specimens that the team collects include saliva, skin cells, blood, fingerprints, and footprints. They examine all of these components to determine the how, why, and ultimately who committed the crime. My favorite part of the examination of the specimens is when the investigators use an element called Luminal. This liquid is an extremely sensitive formula that reacts to blood. They spray this onto an area of the crime scene, like carpet or walls, that appears to be clean, and then they turn off all the lights. The investigators then turn on a special blue light and reexamine the same area. Any remnants of blood glow under the blue light. Blood splatter and blood patterns that were not visible under the regular light are exposed. It is always amazing to see the blood splatter and patterns revealed when put under the blue light.

 This same application is true in our own lives. Upon reexamining our lives, we have sins, past hurts, disappointments, and pains we have attempted to cover up. We think they are cleaned up and covered over and are no longer visible. But when we shine His light upon those areas, we can see that they are still there. We see that they actually are not covered up or cleaned up as we had thought. But through the light of His love, we see something amazing. We see the hurts, pains, and "crimes" of our past in a new light and this time there is a new blood splatter. The sins of our past are covered in the blood of Jesus. His blood shines brightly over all of our past shame and guilt when His love is the light through which we view our past. Additional evidence of God's presence in our lives is able to be seen as well. Just as the investigators at the crime scene collect evidence of footprints, we are able to see God's footprints in our lives. One of my favorite poems, "Footprints" by Mary Fishback, talks about how, as we walk along the beach of our lives, we will see two sets of footprints: ours and God's. But during our struggles and sufferings in life, we will only see one set of footprints; those of God's, for it is during those times that He carries us. I believe when we view our lives through the light of God's love, His footprints will shine even brighter. His fingerprints are evident all over our lives as well. As we look back over our lives, we can discern certain times and situations in which God protected, led, provided for, and even directed us in certain ways. Just as our fingerprints are unique to each of us, the manner in which He does each of these things in our lives is just as unique. God's fingerprint on our lives is a unique pattern distinctive to each one of us. As we reexamine our lives by shining His light on our past, we are able to view our lives as they were intended to be seen: through the filter of His love and covered in His blood. Reexamining our past through God's light and love enables us to not only see things in a different light but allows us to live today knowing that His blood, footprints, and fingerprints are evident in our daily walk with Him.

Daily Scriptures
Monday
Psalm 26:2 KJV "Examine me, O Lord, and prove me; try my reins and my heart."

How can I ask the Lord to examine my heart and what will I do when He answers?

Tuesday
Psalm 139: 23-24 ESV "Search me, O God, and know my heart! Try me and know my thoughts! And see if there be any grievous way in me and lead me in the way everlasting!"

Is there anything in my heart that grieves the Lord and if so what do I need to change?

Wednesday
Lamentations 3:40 KJV "Let us search and try our ways, turn again to the Lord."

How can I search my ways and turn to the Lord, in every area of my life?

Thursday
Romans 8:1 KJV "There is therefore now no condemnation to them which are in Christ Jesus, who walk not after the flesh, but after the Spirit."

How am I walking after the Holy Spirit and not in the flesh, living without condemnation in my life?

Friday

1 Thessalonians 5:21-22 NET "But examine all things; hold fast to what is good. Stay away from every form of evil."

How am I examining the things in my life to ensure I am holding onto what is good and staying away from what is evil?

Weekly Wrap Up

Re-examine redefined:

How can I apply this to my daily life?

Week
32

Real

Real

Adjective

Definition – occurring in fact, actually existing, not artificial
Synonym – authentic, genuine

What is real? When I try to define this word, I have to examine my life, my relationships, my faith, and ultimately what I can actually relate to as real in my life. In attempting to define what is real, my first thoughts are to compare and contrast other things in my world. For instance, is what I see on social media real or have the photos been filtered, altered, taken at another time? Has the poster waited for the perfect time to post? Are the smiles real? Backgrounds staged? What is real? And what can be said about my own life?

When we are attempting to define what is real, especially in our own lives, we can't compare ourselves with others. We are not called to judge their lives. Comparing our lives with others can lead to feelings of inferiority or pride. We are all gifted in unique ways, walking on tailor-made paths designed by God. But we are called to have our own faith, not the faith of our parents, spouse, or our friends. 2 Cor. 13:5 says we are to examine ourselves to see if our faith is real. First and foremost what is real in our lives must be our faith. If our faith is not real, then really nothing else matters. We need to know what we believe and why we believe it. We can not be someone we are not. We need to know who we are and who we are not. Knowing what we believe and why will determine who we are and who we are not. Writing down your beliefs, knowing your morals, standards, and values will enable you to know who you are and more importantly who are not. These standards will allow you to know what you stand for, which is so important because as the old saying goes, "If you do not stand for something, you will fall for anything and everything."

There are a lot of counterfeit things in our culture. We have counterfeit money, handbags, jewelry, electronics, and apparel such as clothing and shoes. It is getting more and more difficult to discern the real items from the fake. We have to decipher everyday information that is given to us and ascertain whether it is real or not. The authenticity of things all around us is beyond questionable. The filters through which we decipher the world around us is crucial. Our primary filter should always be God's word. This may not seem so important when buying a new purse, but when interpreting information, it is critical.

One of the most important things in our culture is love. Finding real, authentic love is special and amazing. Sadly, so many people in our society look for real love and affirmation in counterfeit places. Some people believe that real love comes from alcohol, drugs, a number on a scale, removing all their wrinkles, getting a smaller nose, gambling, sex, shopping, you name it. All of these counterfeit options will never fill the real void that only God can provide. His love is the only thing that is absolutely real, 100 percent of the time. It is authentic and can be trusted. Being real with ourselves involves realizing that He is what we need. Only God can provide the love that we are searching for to fill the void that lies within us.

One of my favorite books is *The Velveteen Rabbit* by Margery Williams. In this children's book, Williams chronicles a stuffed rabbit and his desire to become real through the love of his owner. The rabbit finally surmises what being real actually looks like. "You become. It takes a long time. That is why it doesn't happen often to people who break easily or have sharp edges, or who must be carefully kept. Generally, by the time you are Real, most of your hair has been loved off, and your eyes drop out and you get loose in the joints and very shabby. But these things don't matter at all because once you are Real you can't be ugly, except to people who don't understand."

Daily Scriptures
Monday
1 John 3:18 ESV "Little children, let us not love in word or talk but in deed and in truth."
How am I loving others authentically, not just with my words, but in deed and truth?

Tuesday
Matthew 7:20 NET "So then, you will recognize them by their fruit."
What is the fruit that others recognize in my life?

Wednesday
1 Corinthians 11:1 NET "Be imitators of me, just as I also am of Christ."
How am I imitating Christ in my daily life?

Thursday
Proverbs 27:19 NLT "As a face is reflected in water, so the heart reflects the real person."
How does my heart reflect who I truly am?

Friday

John 8:32 NLT "And you will know the truth, and the truth will set you free."

How does knowing the reality of God's love set me free in my daily life?

Weekly Wrap Up

Real redefined:

How can I apply this to my daily life?

Week
33

Recognize

Recognize

Verb

Definition – identify someone or something from a previous encounter

Synonym – acknowledge, know

Caller ID is one of the greatest inventions of modern times. I am old enough to remember a time when the phone would ring, and a person had no idea who was on the other end of the line before answering. A person had to answer the phone in order to find out who was calling. What a concept. Today, the caller's name and phone number are displayed on the screen at the time of the call. And if the display indicates "unknown caller" then the person has the option of disregarding the call. But prior to caller ID, a person typically relied on recognizing the voice of the person on the other end of the phone. Sometimes the caller would identify themselves, but for the most part, it was up to the person to recognize the caller. And there are certain friends and family members that, quite frankly, do not require caller ID today—we are able to recognize their voices as soon as they begin to speak. They have a very distinctive voice, and we talk so often that I recognize their voice immediately. My parents are two such people. I am extremely fortunate to still have both of my parents alive and I can recognize their voices on the telephone, in a crowded restaurant or across a stadium for that matter. I have known them for so long and talk with them often; I recognize their voices automatically.

John 10:27 says, "My sheep know my voice, and they listen and follow me." All through the Bible, as Christ's followers, we are referred to as His sheep. The more time we spend in prayer and His word, the more we will be able to recognize God's voice. Just as we spend time with our family and friends and can recognize their voices, the more time we spend with God, we learn to discern and recognize His voice. And as we grow closer to Him, we recognize Him at work in our lives as well. We begin to see how He answers our prayers, often times in unexpected ways and ways other than we asked, but still, He answers them. We begin to recognize His hand at work in our lives as we see Him moving and working, but it all begins with spending time with Him and learning to recognize His voice. God speaks in many different ways. Primarily He speaks to us through His word. He speaks to us through prayer, through Godly people in our lives, through dreams and visions, and through the still small voice. God will choose to speak to us in any way He wants. The question is, are we listening, and will we recognize His voice when He chooses to speak to us? We cannot limit God and how He speaks, but we must always be ready to answer His call and recognize His voice when He does call.

I am blessed to have three daughters. Although their primary means of communication with me is through text messaging, they do call me, which I absolutely love. And although I am grateful for the afore- mentioned caller ID, this is another time that it is not necessary. I can recognize their voices immediately. I am able to distinguish between their voices immediately by the way they say "Mom." I can not only distinguish between their voices, but I can also determine their moods. I am able to recognize a troubled "Mom" and distinguish that from an elated "Mom!" Distinguishing voices is critical in a mother's life but also in our spiritual life. We must know and recognize the voice of God easily to be able to distinguish when the enemy comes calling. And he will. He tries to fill our head with all kinds of craziness. The enemy will tell us lies: *You're not good enough, not smart enough, and unworthy. You will never overcome that sin in your life. You have to be perfect to come to God. Oh, that sin is no big deal. You need to handle that little problem yourself. You are all alone. No one else has ever felt like this. God cannot be good all the time. You could never do anything great for the kingdom of God.* And the most ridiculous: the enemy is someone you should be afraid of. If we are not able to distinguish the voice of God from the lies of the enemy, we just might believe some of these lies. We must recognize them for what they are—complete and total attacks, falsehoods, and assaults on our minds. The enemy does not want us to flourish and thrive. Jesus came that we may have life and have it more abundantly (John 10:10) We simply need to recognize God's voice and distinguish it from the enemy's.

Knowing that God came to give us life more abundantly, we can trust that He wants and knows what is best for us. We need to recognize God's best. Living according to His Spirit, we will not settle for doing God's good in our lives. Being led by His Spirit allows us to recognize God's best. We are not called to do everything for God, but we are called to do only what He says. This is one reason it is crucial to recognize and obey His voice. He also leads us to recognize sin in our lives in order for us to confess and repent of that sin. When we recognize God's voice, we can live according to the calling He has placed on our lives, obeying His word, following His lead, living in the abundance of His goodness, grace, and power.

Daily Scriptures
Monday

Philippians 1:9-10 NLT "For I want you to understand what really matters, so that you may live pure and blameless lives until the day of Christ's return."

How can I recognize what really matters in my life so that I may live a blameless and pure life?

Tuesday

Matthew 5:16 NLT "In the same way, let your good deeds shine out for all to see, so that everyone will praise your heavenly Father."
How can others recognize Christ through my good deeds so that they give Him the glory and praise?

Wednesday

John 10:14 NLT "I am the good shepherd; I know my own sheep, and they know me."
How can I recognize God's voice in my life?

Thursday

Philippians 4:5 "Let your gentleness be evident to all. The Lord is near."
Is God's gentleness recognizable to all in my life? If not, what can I change to make it so?

Friday

1 John 3:16 "This is how we know what love is: Jesus Christ laid down his life for us. And we ought to lay down our lives for our brothers and sisters."
How is God's love recognizable to others in my life?

Weekly Wrap Up

Recognize redefined:

How can I apply this to my daily life?

Week
34

Reverse

Reverse

Verb

Definition – to move backward, complete change of direction

Synonym – opposite, contrary

My dad began teaching me to drive when I was 13 years old. Although the legal driving age is 15 for a driving permit and 16 for a driver's license, he thought the more I practiced, the better prepared I would be when the time to drive solo arrived. If truth be told, he actually began teaching to drive even earlier. I would sit in his lap even before my little legs could reach the gas or brake pedals. He would allow me to steer the wheel for short increments of time in abandoned parking lots. We would then graduate to longer stints of my hands on the wheel versus his hands on the wheel. This progressed until it was time to allow me to sit in the driver's seat alone, not in his lap but with him in the passenger seat beside me. Before actually turning on the ignition, my dad went through all the pre-driving steps. Check your mirrors, and put on your seat belt; is your seat too close to the steering wheel or too far away? I felt sure there were fewer pre-launch steps to launch Apollo 13 to the moon, but I complied and followed all of his orders. But I will never forget one of his directives as it applies to not only driving a car, but to life as well. He told me as we sat in a parking spot preparing to drive, to shift the car into reverse, that I needed to look back, not just in the rearview mirror but over my shoulder as well. He said there are times when we need to go in reverse and back up in order to go forward. He said just like that parking spot, we can get stuck and the only way to get out is in reverse. Going in reverse is not always a bad thing. Sometimes it is the only way to go. I have remembered that not only in driving but in my life as well. As I taught my three daughters to drive, I passed along this piece of critical advice. We will get in situations where backing up is not only okay but necessary. Sometimes the only way out is to go backward in the direction that we came from, so we can begin again. We need to look over our shoulder and see where we may have made a wrong turn or gone in a wrong direction. We simply need to reverse back to where we strayed off the path and begin again. The good news is that we never stray so far that we cannot reverse course and begin again. And just like the parking spot, what may seem like a stagnant place with no way forward, may just be an opportunity for little step backward so that we can move ahead with God.

My dad passed along a lot of insight while teaching me to drive. I am not sure if he was aware at the time that he was teaching more than how to drive a car. Looking back now, I am positive he knew what he was doing. He was great at capitalizing on opportunities to use teaching moments. He showed me that cars have two pedals: a gas and a brake. Seems obvious, I know. The gas pedal is intended to make us go and the car cannot go unless we use it, but we need to be careful with this pedal because it is extremely powerful. We can press the gas too hard and go so fast that we drive out of control and wreck. The same is true in our lives. If we are not careful with how fast or recklessly, we live, we can crash, burnout, or hurt others in the process. But just as our car has a gas pedal, our cars and our lives are equipped with a brake pedal. We cannot drive or live without brakes. We must know how and when to apply the brakes. We need to know in our lives when it is time to take a "break" and slow down. There could be an upcoming turn in the road ahead, fog that makes it difficult to see, or an obstacle in the road that we are unaware of, and we need to apply the brakes and slow down.

Our lives have a lot of similarities to driving a car. I am thankful that my dad took the time to teach me with patience and insight and I pray I did the same with my daughters. I also believe that when we get in the car every morning, it becomes second nature and maybe we do not go through all of our pre-launch sequences like we did when we first began to drive. However, in life, we need to start our day with a few pre-launch sequences before we just take off and start driving. We need to put on our seatbelt and make sure we are safe and secure for the day. Putting on the armor of God (Ephesians 6:10-18) discusses the details that we are called to put on daily and one of them is the belt of truth. When we are secure in God's truth and allow His truth to drive our lives, we can rest in the security that He will direct us where we need to go. We should also check our mirrors and see what is around us. What are we looking at? What are we allowing to be poured into our minds through our eyes? What our eyes see is what fills our minds and hearts. By checking our mirrors, we are making sure that what is around us is pure, true, honest, lovely, good, and worthy to be praised. (Phil. 4:8) These are the types of things that should be in our mirrors when we check them before launching out for the day. And finally, when we put the key in the ignition to drive off for the day, we need to understand that the driving force for our lives is God's love. That is the key that makes our lives go and work as they are intended. Without the key of God's love, we will stay in the garage of our lives. Oh we might actually drive our cars but not filled with the power and potency that God intended them to have. And we need His love to drive our lives in such a way that we remain on the roads that God directs so we can merge with other drivers. God is the ultimate GPS that helps us to navigate the best route, avoiding traffic jams, and providing directions along our route. Occasionally we hit potholes or miss an exit but there is always beautiful scenery to be viewed if we simply slow down and breathe. The beauty is in the journey. We know our final destination and can trust that God will bring us home at the end of our journey, safe and sound, and right on time.

Daily Scriptures
Monday
Ephesians 6:13 "Therefore put on the full armor of God, so that when the day of evil comes, you may be able to stand your ground, and after you have done everything, to stand."

What does it mean for me to put on the whole armor of God?

Tuesday
Ephesians 6:14 "Stand firm then, with the belt of truth buckled around your waist, with the breastplate of righteousness in place."

How does wearing the belt of truth impact my daily life?

Wednesday
Philippians 4:8 "Finally, brothers and sisters, whatever is true, whatever is noble, whatever is right, whatever is pure, whatever is lovely, whatever is admirable—if anything is excellent or praiseworthy—think about such things."

How can I focus more on these things in my life?

Thursday
Jeremiah 3:22 NLT "My wayward children," says the LORD, come back to me, and I will heal your wayward hearts."

How do I view going in reverse in my life? Do I see it as necessary at times or always as a negative?

Friday

Romans 8:28 "And we know that in all things God works for the good of those who love him, who[a] have been called according to his purpose."

How can I apply this verse to my life, even when I view going in reverse to move forward as a negative?

Weekly Wrap Up

Reverse redefined:

How can I apply this to my daily life?

Week
35

Reflection

Reflection

Noun

Definition – an image seen in a mirror or shiny surface

Synonym – image, resemblance

Mirrors are all around us. They are an essential part of life whether we like it or not. We use them to apply makeup in the morning, fix our hair, check out an outfit, try on swimsuits and blue jeans, and even check to see if we have something stuck in our teeth. Mirrors are essential. I have seen a few people at times and wondered if they own a mirror with some of the color combinations they are wearing, but for the most part, we use them every day. There are times we may attempt to avoid mirrors. For instance, when we first step out of the shower prior to grabbing our towel or first thing in the morning while we still exhibit "bedhead."

Mirrors have been around for years, if not for centuries. There are references throughout history and the Bible of people using different objects as mirrors. Anything from polished metal or polished stone to glass and water were used as ways of looking at one's reflection. Scripture discusses mirrors in Exodus 38:8, "Moreover, he made the laver of bronze with its base of bronze, from mirrors of the serving women who served at the doorway of the meeting." And Proverbs 27:19, "As in water face reflects face, so the heart of man reflects man." But James 1:23 discusses an analogy as to how we should view a mirror. "For if anyone is a hearer of the word and not a doer, he is like a man who looks at his natural face in a mirror, for once he has looked at himself and gone away, he has immediately forgotten what kind of person he was." James is expressing a powerful insight in this verse. Merely glancing or looking at God's word is not enough. We cannot only look and without retaining what we see, or read in this case. If we glance at God's word or hear it and do not apply it to our lives and allow it to affect our actions, then it is like looking at ourselves in a mirror and then immediately forgetting what we look like. That should not be possible. We need to take careful consideration to hear, read, see, and perceive what God is revealing to us so that we take action and do what His word says to do.

Some of us have a love/hate relationship with mirrors. There are people who take their relationship with mirrors to an extreme and fall in love with what they see in the mirror. The term for these people is narcissists. This term comes from a Greek myth about Narcissus. He was a young, attractive guy who fell in love with his own reflection in a pool of water. Narcissists tend to have an extremely high sense of importance and entitlement, need constant praise and attention, frequently put others down to make themselves feel better, and exaggerate their importance. They typically love to look at themselves in the mirror, take lots of selfies and frequently post on social media everything they do because they assume everyone wants to know their every move. On the flip side of the coin are those with extremely low self-esteem and low self-worth. These people typically have a fear of being special, or standing out in any way, are extremely sensitive to others' needs and focus on other people rather than themselves. They absolutely never ask for help, blame themselves for the world's problems, and do not have their own ideas, opinions, or beliefs. These people are typically called echoes as they live their lives as an echo of someone else's life. They avoid mirrors at all costs and are only in pictures if someone else posts them on social media.

So, what is the happy medium between narcissists and echoes? Neither one of these extremes are healthy. Mirrors are not our enemy. We have already established that we need them, even if only to get the spinach out of our teeth. We need them for what they were intended to be used for in the first place. 2 Corinthians 3:18 says, "But we all, with unveiled face, beholding as in a mirror the glory of the Lord, are being transformed in the same image from glory to glory, just as from the Lord, the Spirit." We can behold God's glory today, but not with our natural eyes or face to face. Not yet. But we can behold His glory with the eyes of our heart. It is like looking in a mirror. When we look in a mirror, we are only seeing a reflection of ourselves. We are still not seeing our actual selves, merely a reflection. That is how we can view God's glory today, simply as a reflection. And for other people in our lives to see His glory, they must see it reflected through our lives. They cannot see Him face to face either, so they are dependent upon us to reflect His image. And the more we transform ourselves into His likeness, the more others are able to see God. Our goal is to look more and more like Jesus. When we look in the mirror, it is not to see if we have lost weight, have more wrinkles than yesterday, or if these jeans make us look fat. We should look in the mirror for a couple of reasons: to reflect back on our past and all the wonderful things that God has done for us and to see how far we have come in transforming into His image. We will never get there while we are still here on earth, but we should strive to look more and more like Him every day. And as the image in the mirror reflects, may it reveal that we are a little closer today than we were yesterday.

Daily Scriptures
Monday

James 1:23-27 "Anyone who listens to the word but does not do what it says is like someone who looks at his face in a mirror and, after looking at himself, goes away and immediately forgets what he looks like. But whoever looks intently into the perfect law that gives freedom and continues in it—not forgetting what they have heard but doing it—they will be blessed in what they do."

How can I listen to and read God's word and not forget it, but instead apply it to my daily life?

Tuesday

Proverbs 27:19 "As water reflects the face, so one's life reflects the heart."

How does my life reflect what is in my heart?

Wednesday

1 Corinthians 13:12 "For now we see only a reflection as in a mirror; then we shall see face to face. Now I know in part; then I shall know fully, even as I am fully known."

How do I imagine it will be when I see the Lord face to face?

Thursday

2 Corinthians 3:18 "And we all, who with unveiled faces contemplate the Lord's glory, are being transformed into his image with ever-increasing glory, which comes from the Lord, who is the Spirit."

In what specific ways am I being transformed into God's image?

Friday

1 John 5:7 "But if we walk in the light, as he is in the light, we have fellowship with one another, and the blood of Jesus, his Son, purifies us from all sin."

How can I reflect God's light to those around me today?

Weekly Wrap Up

Reflection redefined:

How can I apply this to my daily life?

Week
36

Ready

Ready

Adjective
Definition – all set, organized, put together
Synonym – prepared, equipped, primed

"Are you ready yet?" "We need to go, now!" I have lost count how many times I have said these words, yelled them actually, up the stairs to my three daughters as we hurried out the door. As they finished putting on makeup or the perfect outfit, gathering their backpacks, shoes, and belongings for the day, I stand at the stairs with car keys in hand, rushing them out the door. To their credit, they are great girls. They just happen to be daughters of a mother who prefers to be early everywhere she goes, so they must be early as well. They have acquired this trait growing up. Although being early to appointments, practices, and school is typically easy to manage schedule-wise, it is not an easy lifestyle to control in my spiritual life. It has been said that patience is a virtue, however my ability to wait without agitation or frustration needs some work.

God prepares our character to match our calling in life. We may believe that we are ready for what He is calling us to do, but it will only succeed on His timetable. For example, Moses had a tremendous call on his life. God had placed such a significant call on his life that he needed time to develop his character to match the calling. Moses was 40 years old, shepherding the sheep of his father-in-law on the backside of the wilderness when God appeared to him. God did not appear to Moses in Pharaoh's palace, in the temple, or even in his tent. God chose the very place that Moses seemed to be the most discontent with his life and current situation, the backside of the wilderness. There are times in our lives when we are discontent with our lives, our jobs, maybe even our marriages and think there is no possible way that God could use us or our situation for His benefit or glory. And that is the exact moment and place that God chooses to meet us, speak to us, and turn our dissatisfaction into a mountaintop moment. He knows the exact moment we are ready for an encounter with Him. It is not when we think we are ready, but when He decides we are. God chooses when and where to meet us, and sometimes it is on the backside of the wilderness in places of discontent. Moses could have attempted to run ahead of God, tapped his foot, or looked at his sundial and wondered when and where is God? But Moses continued to do his work and waited, and God showed up.

God waited not only for the perfect geographical conditions to call Moses, but He also wanted the conditions of his heart to be right as well. When God called Moses from the bush (Exodus 3:2-5) Moses responded with, "Here I am." This response has more to do with his availability than stating his location. In order for God to send Moses on his intended mission (to rescue the Israelites from Egypt and bring them back to the land God had promised Abraham), God required that Moses know Who was talking to him and ready Moses for the journey ahead. Moses would need some reassurance and confirmation in the process, but all of this was part of Moses' preparation. There are times in life when we think we are ready prior to the time that God knows we are. And there are other times that God knows we are ready for our calling, and we don't yet think we are ready. Either way, we must align our timetable with God's schedule. This was a time that Moses had been prepared by God and was ready to step into his calling. He needed assurance from God, but God knew he was ready. Staying on God's timetable is always the most secure way to live our lives.

God has always used the question, *Are you ready?* in powerful and momentous ways in my life. He has asked me this question on more than one occasion, but I know when He asks that something profound is about to happen. I need to be on the lookout even more than usual for His hand to move in a distinctive way in my life. Likewise, I believe that we must ready ourselves for whatever God brings to us. The primary ways in which we ready ourselves are through prayer, reading His word, spending quiet time listening for Him to lead and direct us, being engaged at church with other believers, and through worship. When we seek Him with all of our hearts (Deuteronomy 4:29) we will find Him, and He will prepare us and ready us for our calling and purpose. And unlike the times I stand at the bottom of the stairs yelling, "Are you ready?" at my daughters so we can leave the house, He is never impatient with us. He uses our circumstances to prepare and ready us in a way that aligns with His timetable. So when He does call to us when can answer, "Here I am Lord. Send me."

Daily Scriptures
Monday

Matthew 24:44 "So you also must be ready, because the Son of Man will come at an hour when you do not expect him."

What will change in my life today as I live "ready" for the return of Christ at any moment?

Tuesday

1 Peter 3:15 NLT "Instead, you must worship Christ as Lord of your life. And if someone asks about your hope as a believer, always be ready to explain it."

Am I ready to explain the hope I have in Jesus? If not, what can I do to be ready to share my hope as a believer with others?

Wednesday

Psalm 46:1 NLT "God is our refuge and strength, always ready to help in times of trouble."

What does it mean to me to know that God is always ready to help me when I am in trouble?

Thursday

1 Corinthians 16:13 CEV "Keep alert. Be firm in your faith. Stay brave and strong."

How am I being prepared and ready, staying firm and strong in my daily walk with Christ?

Friday

1 Peter 5:8 NLT "Stay alert! Watch out for your great enemy, the devil. He prowls around like a roaring lion, looking for someone to devour."

How am I staying ready and alert against the enemy's schemes in my life?

Weekly Wrap Up

Ready redefined:

How can I apply this to my daily life?

Week
37

Replace

Replace

Verb

Definition – to put something back where it belongs

Synonym – exchange, substitute

Our lives are filled with items that we need to replace. These objects are all around us and require our attention, sometimes daily. Our society is overflowing with things that are disposable and easy to replace, rather than long-term items that necessitate maintenance and care. The former are cheaply made while the latter require more of an investment. For instance, paper plates, paper towels, plastic cups, bottled water, shaving razors, light bulbs, contact lenses, toothbrushes, toilet paper, diapers, and ink cartridges are all disposable. Some of these do not have a long-term alternative, but all of them require that we replace them on a regular basis. Thankfully, we do not have reusable toilet paper—but replacing the toilet paper roll is a necessity. The things we tend to dispose of and replace so easily are not meant for long-term use. Paper plates and plastic cups are not as valuable as our grandmother's heirloom China and crystal stemware. The plastic, disposable flatware does not have as much meaning as the flatware that has been in our family for generations. These items carry with them cherished memories and are generational treasures that cannot be replaced.

However there are some things in our lives that we need to replace. While we are not called to live a disposable lifestyle when it comes to our emotions or feelings, there are a few things that do need replacing.

The first is our heart of stone, to be replaced with a heart of flesh. Ezekiel 36:26 says, "And I will give you a new heart and put a new spirit within you and I will remove the heart of stone from your flesh and give you a heart of flesh." God never takes something away without replacing it with something better. When He takes away the heart of stone, he replaces it with His Spirit (Ezekiel 36:27) and cause them to come to life (Ezekiel 37:14). The things God replaces are far better than what He removed.

We need to replace negativity in our lives with a positive outlook. The words we choose to speak have tremendous power. "The tongue has the power of life and death," says Proverbs 18:21. If we are speaking negative, harmful, belittling words about ourselves, then it is no wonder that our lives are filled with death and destruction. You may think that is an overstatement but re-read Proverbs 18:21. We need replace our words with what God says and it all begins with two things. What we read and put into our minds, as well as what we think and believe. Prosperous, powerful, positive women spend time daily in the word of God soaking up His life-changing promises. They in turn speak those promises over their lives and the lives of their family, friends, and love ones. For example, 1 Peter 2:9 says that you are a chosen people, a royal priesthood, and God's special possession. Chosen means that He chose you. You are not disposable. You are a treasured heirloom that He chose on purpose for a purpose. You are like fine China that is meant to be cherished and adored for generations. You are not a single-use paper plate that ends up in the trash after one function. There are many promises to speak over yourself. "I am fearfully and wonderful made" (Psalm 139:14). "I am blessed and highly favored" (Luke 1:28). "My words are anointed" (Psalm 45:2). "No weapons formed against me will prosper" (Isaiah 54:17). "I am renewed" (Isaiah 40:31). " I am a new creature" (2 Corinthians 5:17). "I will bear much fruit" (John 15:5). "I am the head and not the tail, above and not beneath" (Deuteronomy 28:13). "I do not have a spirit of fear but of power, love and a sound mind" (2 Timothy 1:7). "I am anointed of God" (1 John 2:27). These are just a few positive promises from God's word that you can begin to speak and pray over yourself, your family, and your loved ones.

As you do so, do not be surprised when you begin to see radical changes in your attitude, your outlook on life, and in your life.

Another needful replacement in your life is to begin to replace an attitude of apathy with thankfulness and gratitude. When you begin to appreciate life and everything in it, you find that you are grateful for your health, relationships, your job, your family, your friends, your home, and more. You begin to view everything around you through a gratitude lens. It requires that a person make the conscious effort to shift the focus from themselves onto someone else or something else. When you cultivate an attitude of gratitude, you develop a habit of looking for the best in a situation, and that coincides with becoming a more positive person. People tend to find what they look for, whether that is their lost keys, a cell phone, or the good in life. If you look for the bad, you will almost always find it. If you search for the good in a situation, you will almost always find that as well. Replacing the search for the negative with looking for the positive allows a heart of gratitude to naturally fall into place. Practicing gratitude (it will require some practice at first) will bring a sense of contentment and enjoyment to your life that may have been missing. When you begin to express your thankfulness to others, it will rub off on the people around you. Days may not always be great, but there is always something great to find in every day. Once you develop this mindset, you cannot help but spread this contagious attitude to others as you spend time thanking the people in your life. Consider the people you see on a daily or weekly basis. Who would you rather spend time with? The person who brings the mood up in a room, who is always grateful for life and is telling you about how wonderful their day is? Or the person who drags the mood down every time you see them? The gloom and doom looks for the bad, ungrateful Eeyore who searches out the negativity in life. You already know the answer, so be the sunshine-spreading, gratitude-sharing person that others need in their life. 1 Thesselonians 5:16-18 says, "Rejoice always, pray continually, give thanks in all circumstances; for this is God's will for you in Christ Jesus." This is my life verse. We are called to give thanks *in* all circumstances. It does not say to give thanks *for* all circumstances. Not everything that happens to us is going to be great. We cannot be thankful for everything. However, we are called to be thankful in all things.

 Finally, in our disposable, plastic world, there are things that I believe cannot be replaced. Just as we have paper napkins and plastic cups, we also have crystal stemware and priceless antiques that cannot be replaced. I have a china cabinet that is filled with such items. I have many family treasures that cannot be replaced. One item is a pitcher and cups from Italy that my grandfather brought back after fighting in WWII. He carefully wrapped these priceless treasures in his duffle bag and carried them back to my grandmother. My grandfather has since passed away, but these treasures are a sweet reminder of not only his love for my grandmother and how he thought of her while overseas, but also of the love he had for his country. I also have teacups and saucers from my other grandmother. These delicate porcelain treasures are sweet reminders of how fragile life can be. A few of these teacups have been chipped over the years and required mending, but they will never be discarded or replaced. They serve as a reminder that God uses broken things too. We are all broken. We all need a little mending over the years but that mending never diminishes our worth, value, or beauty. We are all beautiful and useful to God and cannot be replaced. Just like my precious family heirlooms in my china cabinet, we are all valuable, beautiful, and irreplaceable. We have cracks and chips, but these are the exact spots where God is able to shine from within us. It is through the brokenness that He is able to shine the brightest. And rather than tossing us away because of that brokenness, God says we cannot be replaced. We are valuable. We are His and we are worthy to be called irreplaceable.

Daily Scriptures
Monday
Ezekiel 36:26 NLT "And I will give you a new heart, and I will put a new spirit in you. I will take out your stony, stubborn heart and give you a tender, responsive heart."

What does it look like in my life that God has replaced my stony stubborn heart with a tender, responsive heart?

Tuesday
2 Corinthians 5:17 "Therefore, if anyone is in Christ, the new creation has come: The old has gone, the new is here!"

How has my old self been replaced through my relationship with Christ?

Wednesday
Philippians 4:8 "Finally, brothers and sisters, whatever is true, whatever is noble, whatever is right, whatever is pure, whatever is lovely, whatever is admirable—if anything is excellent or praiseworthy—think about such things."

What are some practical ways I can replace my old thoughts with the things listed in this verse?

Thursday
Ephesians 4:21-24 "when you heard about Christ and were taught in him in accordance with the truth that is in Jesus. You were taught, regarding your former way of life, to put off your old self, which is being corrupted

by its deceitful desires; to be made new in the attitude of your minds; and to put on the new self, created to be like God in true righteousness and holiness."

What are some ways I can replace my old sinful nature and deceitful desires with my new life in Christ?

Friday

Colossians 3:12 "Therefore, as God's chosen people, holy and dearly loved, clothe yourselves with compassion, kindness, humility, gentleness and patience."

What behaviors in my life need to be replaced with the ones listed in this verse? What are some practical ways I can do this in my daily life?

Weekly Wrap Up

Replace redefined:

How can I apply this to my daily life?

Week
38

Rearrange

Rearrange

Verb
Definition – move around, arrange differently
Synonym – reposition, reorganize, alter, adjust

We moved into a new home several years ago. We lived in the home prior to this new home for almost 20 years. Prior to the move, we needed to complete a thorough elimination of clutter and excess that we had accumulated over the years. The new house required some new furniture for a few rooms that the old house did not have. While that was fun to shop for at the time, the placement and arrangement of the furniture became stressful because I know myself; once the furniture has been placed, it will not be moved. I am not one for rearranging furniture. I like things to stay as they are and everything to be in its place. I do not mind adding a few decorations here and there, but rearranging furniture is not in my comfort zone.

I think my life falls into this similar pattern. I like things to remain the same without a lot of rearranging. Once things are in their place, they do not need to be moved. For instance, I do not see the need to rearrange my morning routine. I am set in my ways: I have my quiet time, my breakfast, get ready for work, drive to the same place for coffee every morning, and drive the same exact route to work every morning. I have a routine when I get to work. I have the same routine when I leave work and drive home. I do not see a need to rearrange any of the patterns or routines in my life.

But what if I have arranged my life in a way that does not leave any room for God to move? What if I have "routined" God out of my life? What if I am stuck in a rut and don't even realize it?

In John 5:1-9, we read about a paralyzed man who had been on a mat beside a healing pool in Bethesda for 38 years. Let me repeat, *thirty eight* years. The man had watched as the water stirred, seeing the first person into the stirred water be healed. When Jesus saw this man lying on the mat waiting, He asked the man if he if he wanted to be healed. The man said that others had stepped into the water before him. For 38 years. Jesus told the man to pick up his mat and walk. No excuses. No one was in front of him at this point. The man did not need to wait on the water to be stirred. The man was healed on the spot. Immediately. Did Jesus know this man had become stuck? Did Jesus know that this man was not just physically paralyzed but was also mentally paralyzed? I believe the answer is yes to both of those questions and Jesus knows that one of the greatest dangers in life is when we get stuck in the same-old-same-old. That is how life just passes us by. We are paralyzed by fear, apathy, indifference, or laziness, and we watch as 38 years of our lives pass us by. If we lie on our mat doing nothing for the kingdom, then we are no threat to the enemy. It is safe to stay on the ground, "waiting" for someone else to stir the waters and do the work. Jesus wants to come along and give us no excuse to get up and walk. He wants to rearrange our lives to the point that we are not the same person that we were before we had an encounter with Him. We may like things to be routine, safe, and in their place, but Jesus wants to stir the waters of our heart and cause us to get up, take our mat, and walk. We were not created to be static, powerless, and ineffective. We are called to live our lives in such a way that we are moving forward, fearless in Him.

We must rearrange our lives to make room for the Holy Spirit to move and work. If our lives are too routine and orderly, the Holy Spirit will not have room to act. Think of our lives like a home. Hebrews 4:4 says, "For every house is built by someone but the builder of all things is God." And our bodies are the temple of the Holy Spirit (1 Cor. 6:19) in which He dwells. We need to take care of our bodies, His house, and His temple. We need to let Him rearrange our priorities, our schedule, our purpose, and even our thoughts. (Phil. 4:8) If we allow Him to do the rearranging, then our house will not become a mess. He will put everything where it needs to be.

But we must want to be rearranged. We must answer yes, when Jesus asks the question, *do you want to be healed?* It seemed like such an obvious question when Jesus asks the man lying at the pool at Bethesda. Do we really want our lives to be rearranged or have we settled for lying on a mat for 38 years? Are we comfortable where we are or are we willing to let Jesus rearrange our lives? And what about when He says to get up? What do you think the paralyzed man thought when Jesus said that? It sounded impossible to him I am sure. What will you say when Jesus asks you to attempt the impossible for Him? Will you pick up your mat and walk? Will you let Jesus rearrange your life? The man at the pool at Bethesda had his life completely rearranged. Maybe it is time we allow some rearranging to take place in our lives so we can see the Holy Spirit at work. At His prompting, get out of your rut and attempt the impossible for Him. For if we take up our mats and walk, there is no telling what we can do living a rearranged life.

Daily Scriptures
Monday

Isaiah 43:19 "See, I am doing a new thing! Now it springs up; do you not perceive it? I am making a way in the wilderness and streams in the wasteland."

How am I open to God rearranging the details of my life and doing new things?

Tuesday

Romans 12:2 "Do not conform to the pattern of this world but be transformed by the renewing of your mind. Then you will be able to test and approve what God's will is—his good, pleasing and perfect will."

Am I rearranging my life to conform to the world's pattern for my life or am I being transformed by God's perfect will for me?

Wednesday

Matthew 6:33 "But seek first his kingdom and his righteousness, and all these things will be given to you as well."

How am I rearranging my priorities to seek God's kingdom first in my life?

Thursday

Matthew 6:19 "Do not store up for yourselves treasures on earth, where moths and vermin destroy, and where thieves break in and steal."

What do I need to do to rearrange the treasures in my life, storing them in heaven rather that here on earth?

Friday

John 14:15 "If you love me, keep my commands."

What do I need to rearrange in my life to keep God's commands?

Weekly Wrap Up

Rearrange redefined:

How can I apply this to my daily life?

Week
39

Resist

Resist

Verb

Definition – strive against, to refrain from

Synonym – oppose, withstand

There are quite a few things I cannot resist. A hug from one of my daughters, a bite of chocolate, a great cup of coffee, an extra 10 minutes of sleep, and a quiet night at home with my husband. But there are several things that we as believers are called to resist. The first and I believe the most important thing we are called to resist is the enemy. James 4:7 tells us to, "Resist the devil and he will flee from you." We have been given the power to resist the enemy and his schemes. The beginning of James tells us how. We are called to submit to God. In this powerful act of submission to God and His authority, we align our lives, thoughts, actions, beliefs, and will to His authority, which in turn grows our resistance to the enemy. He must flee as he loses any ground or foothold that he may have in our lives as we submit to God and His authority. While resisting the enemy is the first and most important thing we should resist in our lives,

we should also resist complaining. Philippians 2:14 says, "Do everything without complaining or arguing, so that no one can criticize you. Live clean, innocent lives as children of God, shining like bright lights in a world full of crooked and perverse people." According to this verse, complaining can prevent you from living a life that shines brightly like a star, in contrast to crooked people around you. Complaining does not improve your circumstances and rarely fixes them. When Paul is put in prison and is writing most of the New Testament, he never describes his living conditions. He never describes his cell as damp, smelly, or rat infested. He repeatedly talks about living a life of rejoicing and rejoicing no matter what your circumstances may be. We need to resist complaining at all costs. We need to evaluate the situation and determine if it will really matter in a year, five years or even in five minutes. We should always realize how important what we say is and to whom we say it. People are always watching and listening to us, even when we do not think they are. Are our words bringing others up or are they tearing others down? Are we living life annoyed? Resist complaining and start spreading positive words of encouragement and focus on what is right, rather than what is wrong.

We should also resist trying to control our lives, other people, and every circumstance of our lives. Proverbs 19:21 says, "Many are the plans of man, but the purpose of God will stand." It is a complete waste of time attempting to control other people, their actions, and their responses to us. We need to let go and let God be God. This mindset is easier said than done, but once we realize it is a simpler way to live, it becomes a more peaceful lifestyle as well. We also realize that we are not powerful enough to mess up the plans that God has intended for our lives. He is in charge and try as we may to alter the timing and realization of occurrences in our lives, we will never be God. It is up to Him to say what, when, and how. We just need to resist attempting to control.

I also believe we need to resist being unkind. There are so many people today that have their default set to being mean and having negative reactions. Many people would rather be offended than talk to someone and find out why the person feels the way they do. Some people feel safe posting hateful, unkind words and pictures on social media when they would not say those same things directly to a person's face. Maybe they would. We have so much hate, anger, and unkindness in our world today.

It is so easy to find it. All you have to do is turn on the television or social media. I believe we need to resist being unkind. We need to be the type of people who look for and find the best in others. And when we find it, tell that person and others. Share positive, uplifting, and hopeful ideas. Encourage one another with love and not hate. Do thoughtful deeds and do not tell anyone about it. Bring back random acts of kindness like paying for the person's coffee behind you in the drive-through. We need to resist the temptation to react harshly and unkindly to what we see around us and instead respond to others as we would want to be treated.

Finally, I believe we need to resist judgment and blame. These two words go hand-in-hand. When we judge others, we are evaluating them based primarily on how they look, think, or behave toward us. We typically make a judgement that may or may not consider getting to know the person. "There is only one lawgiver and judge, he who is able to save and to destroy. But who are you to judge your neighbor?" (James 4:12). We are called not to judge ourselves or our neighbor. We should look for the best in ourselves and in our neighbor. The same holds true for casting blame. Matthew 7:3-5 discusses someone observing a speck in another person's eye without acknowledging the log in their own eye. We should not attempt to remove a speck from someone's eye if we are not able to see clearly from a *log* in our own eye. We cannot cast blame on someone else for a fault if we have a fault of our own and since there are no perfect people, then casting blame is useless. Encouraging others, speaking uplifting words, not judging ourselves or casting blame is a simpler, more peaceful way to live.

When we resist these things in our lives, we realize that life becomes more peaceful. Henry David Thoreau said, "It is not what you look at that matters but what you see." When we resist the need to look at what is wrong with our lives and complain about it to others, we begin to live more at ease. We will start to blame others less and stop judging, which will in turn lead to not having to feel in control. All of these things coincide with resisting the enemy. When we submit our lives to God, we are able to see what actually matters in life and live accordingly. And just as Phil. 2:14 says, our lives will shine brightly in a dark world.

Daily Scriptures
Monday
James 4:7 "Submit yourselves, then, to God. Resist the devil, and he will flee from you."

How am I submitting to God and resisting the enemy in my daily life?

Tuesday
1 Peter 5:5 "In the same way, you who are younger, submit yourselves to your elders. All of you, clothe yourselves with humility toward one another, because "God opposes the proud but shows favor to the humble."

Are there any areas of my life where I am proud and need to humble myself towards God?

Wednesday
1 Peter 5:9 "Resist him, standing firm in the faith, because you know that the family of believers throughout the world is undergoing the same kind of sufferings."

How does knowing that other believers undergo the same kind of sufferings as I do help me to resist the enemy?

Thursday
Psalm 119:11 "I have hidden your word in my heart that I might not sin against you."

How does knowing God's word help me to resist temptation and sin?

Friday

Hebrews 4:16 "Let us then approach God's throne of grace with confidence, so that we may receive mercy and find grace to help us in our time of need."

How can I ask God for help in resisting the enemy and temptation?

Weekly Wrap Up

Resist redefined:

How can I apply this to my daily life?

Week
40

Recalculate

Recalculate/Recalculating

Verb
Definition – re-estimate, reconfigure
Synonym – recompute, work-out, deduce

If you ask anyone in my family, they will tell you that one of greatest shortcomings in my life is that I am incredibly directionally challenged. I prefer to view it as a strength–I am extremely qualified at getting lost. Although I have absolutely no sense of direction, I am quite qualified at following the maps app on my phone. I have had several people try to give me directions that include words like southwest, or head east on a certain street, or once you are going north, etc. These words are the equivalent of speaking a foreign language to me. I am however quite capable of following direction that include words like, turn left at the Chick-Fil-A, or turn right at the Exxon gas station, or once you see a Subway, you are almost to your destination. My family knows better than to include directional words in their directions to me.

My daughters have played several sports over the years that involved numerous trips out of town. These precious girls have been incredibly patient as their mom tried to find obscure gyms in new cities. Thankfully, I could not see my daughters roll their eyes as I was too busy trying to read road signs and listen to the GPS direct my next turn. But they could not hide their excitement when Dad was able to go with us on these trips and show off his superior directional skills. For some reason, when he drives, our GPS never says the annoying, yet too familiar words, "Recalculating."

210 - Cyndi Dodson

I have learned to become friends with this word not only when driving, but in my daily life as well. It simply means I have made a wrong turn somewhere along the way and I need to get back on the right path.

There have been many times in my life, not just when taking my daughters to sporting events, that I am certain I am heading the right way, but in actuality I have strayed off the correct course. I am sure the road I am on is the one God wants me to take, and it will eventually lead to the desired destination. However, I am unaware of a roadblock on the road ahead and God knows that I need to recalculate my directions and take another route. Or something happens in our lives like a major life-changing event that seems catastrophic at the time. Our car breaks down and everything comes to a halt. We are forced to recalculate the time that it will take to get to our destination. We think we are off track from where we need to be by a certain time in our lives, but really we are exactly where God wants us to be. God uses all things and all events for His good and for those who love Him. He works everything out for His glory. We may see our broken-down car as a catastrophe when it could really be God's protection.

I have heard the word recalculating more times than I care to remember, but every time it has been a benefit in the long run. The voice on the GPS reminds me that I need get back on course and return to the necessary route. If I continue to stay off course, not only will I remain lost, but I will not arrive at my intended destination. Before I had the GPS app on my phone, I was completely lost. Likewise, before we have Jesus in our lives we are completely lost. If we use anything other than Him for our directions in life, we will remain lost. He knows our exact location no matter how lost we think we are. He is never lost. We will drive through life on various highways and not ever know if we are headed the right way. And without Jesus, we will never reach our ultimate destination, Heaven. He is the voice that speaks to us, like the GPS, that provides directions, warns of upcoming hazards, and helps us stay on the right path. Even when we do not hear Him speak constantly, He is still there. But when we need help and direction, His voice provides the guidance and navigation we need. Then we realize that He has been there all along. Returning to the right path involves spending time in prayer and reading His word. When we consistently do these things and allow Him to speak into our lives, we recalculate our course and set our route on the one true way. The recalculating He provides in our lives allows us not only to get on the right track, but to reach our destination safe and sound. While recalculating may be a word that some of us are not familiar with when driving, it is crucial in our everyday lives as we navigate the twists and turns that could lead off-road. With our Godly GPS, we have the security in knowing we are never lost with Him directing and leading our path.

Daily Scriptures
Monday
Proverbs 16:19 NLT "We can make our plans, but the Lord determines our steps."

What is an instance where God recalculated my plans and my path? Am I open to allowing Him to do it again?

Tuesday
Joshua 3:4 "Then you will know which way to go, since you have never been this way before."

How will I know which way to go in places in my life that I have never been before?

Wednesday

Isaiah 43:2 ESV "When you pass through the waters, I will be with you; and through the rivers, they shall not overwhelm you; when you walk through fire you shall not be burned, and the flame shall not consume you."

When I go through uncharted territory, do I wish that God would recalculate my steps, or do I trust in His faithfulness to lead me safely through the fire?

Thursday

Isaiah 43:19 ESV "Behold, I am doing a new thing; now it springs forth, do you not perceive it? I will make a way in the wilderness and rivers in the desert."

Can I see the new things God is doing in my life? Am I excited about His way in the wilderness, and am I trusting in His direction in my life?

Friday

Isaiah 6:8 ESV "And I heard the voice of the Lord saying, 'Whom shall I send, and who will go for us?' Then I said, 'Here I am! Send me'."

How am I making myself available for God to send me and recalculate my steps in my everyday life?

Weekly Wrap Up

Recalculate redefined:

How can I apply this to my daily life?

Week
41

Relight

Relight

Verb

Definition – to make something burn again

Synonyms – rekindle, reignite, stoke

For as long as I can remember, my mom has collected lighthouses. She has a lighthouse in every room of her house. My mom has lighthouse dishtowels, a lamp, a lighthouse themed bathroom complete with a lighthouse shower curtain and hooks. She has a special collection of a certain type of lighthouses that have been numbered and signed by the artist and for many years, we searched for various lighthouses in this series to complete her collection for Christmas. These lighthouses vary in size, shape, height, color, and design, but each one still carries the same purpose: to shine a beacon of light from a rocky coastline to protect ships, warn of potential hazards, and assist in direction and guidance. These structures have existed for centuries and have been effective in diverting many ships away from danger while illuminating their path to safety. I believe this is the reason my mom is so drawn to lighthouses. Even before becoming a mom, she had an affinity for lighthouses. She did not realize what a beacon of light she would be to me and our family. When she became a mom, her light began to shine even brighter. She stood out on the point, weathered many storms, and let her light shine so I could find my way. I am not sure what I would have done without her guidance in my life.

As my mom shined her light in my life, she illuminated the way for me to see the brightest Light I needed. God sent His Son Jesus into the world, and He is the ultimate light of this world. He is our fundamental source of guidance, strength, and direction. He is our beacon on a hill and we are called to be a city on a hill. In Matthew 5, Jesus is delivered the Sermon on the Mount and discusses how we are called to be salt and light. He says we, as followers of Christ, are the light of this world. He says just as a city on hill cannot be hidden neither do people light a lamp and put it under a bowl. That is not the purpose of the lamp. The purpose of the lamp is to light up the room in which it is sent. The same is true for us. We are to light the dark rooms and places we are placed. Our light should shine so brightly that we extinguish the darkness, no matter where God places us. That could be our jobs, our homes, our city, even our church. In the climate of our current culture, the darkness of our modern entertainment, social media, politics, and economy, we need light now more than ever. We are called to shine by doing good works not to put the spotlight on ourselves, but to glorify God. Matthew 5:16 says to let our light shine before men so they will see our good deeds and glorify our Father in heaven. But just as our light shines brightly so others will glorify God, our light should also shine as a lighthouse to warn of trouble and looming hazards.

We are called to help others navigate through choppy waters and steer away from jagged shores while pointing them to safety. We are to shine our light through the night and difficult times so others can see through till the morning. But some of us need to relight the flame that lives in us. Just as lighthouses from the past had a lamp lit by fire, we have a fire within us as well. Some of us may need to stoke that fire and rekindle the flame. It is there but may not burn as brightly as it once did. We need to realize that it is not about how good we are that determines how brightly we can shine for Him. No matter what our past looks like, or even what yesterday looks like, we can still shine our light brightly in His name. We need to remember it is His light that shines from within, and it has nothing to do with how good we are or are not. But our world desperately needs us to shine so we need to be willing vessels.

At the end of the day, when we have His light shining from within us, we cannot help but light up the dark places of our lives. Life may try to diminish our sparkle and some days it may seem to win. But we need to remember life is not about what tomorrow brings, but what we bring to tomorrow. We bring Jesus and His light into each and every day. And when we shine for Him, reflecting the light of Christ, we cannot help but relight the world in which we live.

Daily Scriptures
Monday
Matthew 5:14 ESV "You are the light of the world. A city set on a hill cannot be hidden."
How do I keep the light of Jesus shining and unhidden in my life so others can find their way to Him?

Tuesday
Psalm 27:1 ESV "The Lord is my light and my salvation; whom shall, I fear? The Lord is the stronghold of my life; of whom shall I be afraid?"
How does God's light help me to live fearlessly?

Wednesday
Ephesians 5:8 ESV "...for at one time you were darkness, but now you are light in the Lord. Walk as children of light."
What is noticeably different in my life, walking in the light now than when I lived in darkness before becoming a child of God's light?

Thursday

Psalm 119:105 ESV "Your word is a lamp to my feet and a light to my path."

How does God's word illuminate my path?

Friday

Ecclesiastes 2:13 "I saw that wisdom is better than folly, just as light is better than darkness."

How does God's wisdom compare to light?

Weekly Wrap Up

Relight redefined:

How can I apply this to my daily life?

Week
42

Review

Review

Verb

Definition- to look at or examine something again
Synonym- critique, analyze, survey

Throughout my life, I have battled with several different health issues. A couple of these diagnoses were intended to be lifelong challenges and by God's amazing hand, thankfully, I was healed. I struggled a few years ago with an overwhelming bout of double pneumonia and pleurisy. These ailments seemed to go on forever but in actuality it was about six months. There were numerous trips to the emergency room during which I could not get my breath and several times when I was in so much pain I didn't *want* to breathe. We read stories of elderly people passing away from these conditions and now I know why. It seemed I would never get past this season in my life. I just wanted to be able to take a breath and not be in pain. How easy it is sometimes to take the simplest of things for granted, the ability to breathe.

Once I recovered, I promised myself that I would never take the little things in life for granted. I would make a gratitude list and review it often. Reviewing my list led me to re-view my priorities as well. When we view things from a different angle or perspective, we see things in a completely different way. We begin to see everything as a miracle. Albert Einstein said, "There are only two ways to live your life. One is as though nothing is a miracle. The other is as though everything is a miracle." I choose the second option. I choose to re-view everything in my life as a miracle. When we live our lives in this manner, we stop taking the little things in life for granted. We find ourselves not complaining about the challenges we face because we are able to re-view them from a completely different perspective.

In Ezekiel 37:1-14, God revealed that He is the only one that can give dry bones new life. Ezekiel sees in verse 8 that tendons and flesh appear, and skin covers the bones, but there is still no breath in the bones. It is only after God breathes breath into the bones in verse 10 that they live again. This illustration shows God's promise to restore Israel and deliver the nation from their hopeless condition in exile. This vision is also a reminder that whatever I have, large or small, has no worth unless God gives it life. This vision also shows that what I may think is dead, if God wants it alive, He can breathe new life into it. Nothing has life without His breath. This image shared in Ezekiel reminds me that God is the giver of breath.

2 Timothy 3:16 says that all Scripture is breathed out by God. This simply means that His word is active, alive, and relevant to our lives today. Although it was actually penned by imperfect men many years ago with wisdom that has been passed down for generations, the divine nature was inspired by the Holy Spirit. God divinely inspired His word to be written by breathing life into the men who wrote it. Since we have scripture that communicates God's love, direction, counsel and encouragement we can trust that it was inspired by God, know that it is His divine truth, and be assured it can be explored for God's guidance.

As you make a gratitude list and re-view it, I hope you think about the simplest of blessings. Every day is full of gifts and miracles. We may take some of these things for granted because they are just a part of our lives and we have grown accustomed to having them there. But if you wake up, can take a breath, have food on the table, clean water, a home, and can find at least one reason to smile, then you are extremely blessed.

Throughout your daily struggles, challenges, and tests, take a deep breath and thank God for the ability to do so.

Daly Scriptures
Monday
2 Corinthians 4:17 "For our light and momentary troubles are achieving for us an eternal glory that far outweighs them all."

How am I re-viewing my circumstances through the lens of this verse?

Tuesday
Psalm 119:105 "Your word is a lamp for my feet, a light on my path."

How does God's word help me to re-view my life's path?

Wednesday
1 Corinthians 2:9 "However, as it is written: 'What no eye has seen, what no ear has heard, and what no human mind has conceived' the things God has prepared for those who love him."

How does this verse help me to re-view the things of my daily life?

Thursday
Matthew 16:26 "What good will it be for someone to gain the whole world, yet forfeit their soul? Or what can anyone give in exchange for their soul?"

What am I attempting to gain in the world that may be causing me to forfeit my soul? Reviewing this list, what changes do I need to make?

Friday

Isaiah 55:8-9 "'For my thoughts are not your thoughts, neither are your ways my ways,' declares the Lord. As the heavens are higher than the earth, so are my ways higher than your ways, and my thoughts than your thoughts."

How do these verses help me to re-view my circumstances?

Weekly Wrap Up

Review redefined:

How can I apply this to my daily life?

Week
43

Reimagine

Reimagine

Verb

Definition – to think about again, especially to improve it

Synonyms – revisit, re-envision

I really do not care for surprises. Maybe I should reword that – I do not like to be surprised at all. I prefer to know what is going to happen in the next moment, the next hour, and the next week (and year for that matter). I guess you could say I am a planner. I try to plan for the unexpected and unforeseeable in every situation and circumstance. Which, even writing that out sounds odd. If it is unforeseeable, then how is one to plan for it? However, in my simple mind, I attempt to plan for it, because, like I said, I do not like surprises. If you can relate, then can I get an amen? If you have at least considered that something could possibly occur, and it is planned for, then you could not be caught off guard and surprised.

This thought process and way of life is not necessarily healthy, especially when it comes to living a life that is fully reliant upon God. If I am trying to account for every detail and plan every minute of my life, then I have scheduled God right out my life. Being surprised by God, His goodness and faithfulness are surprises that I need to not only allow for in my life, but welcome. When every minute is scheduled, planned, and worried about "what if", then God has no room to work. We cannot plan God. We cannot schedule God, nor should we. We cannot tell God that we are open to visit with Him only on Sundays between 11:00 and 12:00 and then forget about Him the rest of the week. Prisoners in jail get visitation schedules along those lines. We cannot put God in a box and think that He only works in church, only speaks to us in church or only works His precious miracles in church on Sundays. He does do mighty and powerful works in church, but He is so much more outside of the four walls of a building on Sunday mornings. Since His Holy Spirit is alive in us, we take Him everywhere we go. We take Him to our jobs on Monday mornings, to our homes, and to the seedy places we do not like to tell anyone. He is sitting at our kitchen table when we are having difficult conversations with our spouse or our children. And He is just as present there as He is on Sunday morning in the church. We need to reimagine where, how, and when God can work. And we need to reimagine what a surprise looks like, especially from God's perspective.

We can be surprised how and when God chooses to use us. Since He has uniquely gifted each of us, He can choose how to bring about those gifts and talents within us. And it may surprise us when and where they emerge. We need to reimagine what is looks like to be His hands and feet and even His mouth at times. We need to simply be ready when He moves. Ephesians 2:10 says, "We are God's masterpiece created anew in Christ Jesus so we can do the good things that He planned for us long ago." To create a masterpiece takes a lot of forethought, creativity, and unique characteristics. It may surprise you to think about yourself in that way, but you need to reimagine how you see yourself – as God's masterpiece. You were created with careful thought and planning so you can do the good works that He strategically planned long ago. Not what we tried to account for, pre-arrange, or consider that might happen just in case a circumstance arises that we did not foresee occurring. God knows and has the perfect plan. Even if something happens in our lives that we never saw coming, God is never surprised. He works everything out according to His perfect plan and for our good, so although we are surprised, He is not. We simply need to reimagine how we view the unforeseen event and look for how God is going to use that for our good and His glory.

However, when it comes to being surprised, we do not want to be caught off-guard by a surprise attack by the enemy. We need to be alert, prepared, and ready for the enemy's attack in our lives by always putting on the armor of God, as in Ephesians 6. This is not a surprise that anyone wants to experience, but the enemy is always prowling around looking for who he can devour. If we realize that he is real and be on the lookout for and know how he typically likes to attack us, then his attacks will not usually come as such a surprise to us.

Just because we do not like surprises does not mean we do not need them in our lives. We simply need to reimagine how we look at them. Surprises can look like what we would call an interruption but what God calls a divine appointment. In Acts 3, Peter and John are going to the temple to pray when they pass a crippled beggar at the temple gate. Peter and John are interrupted on their way into the temple. The man who has been crippled since birth asks Peter and John for money. But what he received was so much more. Peter and John were open to the interruption and saw the crippled man and stropped what they were doing and where they were going, even to church. Are we open to interruptions? Even if we are going somewhere that we deem important, or that we view as Godly, to be interrupted by God? For God to work a miracle? We need to reimagine what it looks like for God to move and work no matter where we are or what we're doing. This miracle occurred right outside the church. If Peter had given the crippled man the money he asked for, he would have missed his miracle. How many times in our lives has God given us something other than what we asked for in order for us to receive our actual miracle? We need to reimagine our definition of surprise. God answers our prayers not on our timetable but on His schedule. Surprise! When He answers our prayers in His time it is always perfect. But thank God it did not happen when we wanted it to happen because He always knows best. His ways are higher than our ways, and His timing is always better than ours. The crippled man had been sitting at the temple gate for years. God knew exactly when and where to move in his life. If we reimagine what our surprise might look like, when or where it may arrive, then life makes sense and is more peaceful.

So if the crippled man had been sitting at the temple gate for years, I wonder why he was not healed until then? I understand God's perfect timing. But also, could it have been that no one had stopped to talk to him before Peter and John did on that day? How many people passed him all the years he sat at the gate begging? How many people do we pass every day in our lives that are in need? I am not talking about the people who viably hold up signs that say "Help, hungry, need food." Those people are in need too. I am talking about the hurting people all around us that do not hold up visible cardboard signs with their needs, hurts, and wounds written for the world to see. Are we open to be used to help those around us? Do we have the eyes to see those in need? If we do, are we willing to be interrupted and stop and help? Can we reimagine what a surprise looks like and allow God to use us in ways that we may not have imagined? Will we open our hands, mouths, and possibly our hearts to unexpected encounters and be a part of life change? That life change may take place in someone else, and it can even occur within us when we in a constant state of expectation of being surprised. But we must be on the lookout for opportunities each and every day to be used and surprised. If we view each day like Christmas morning, full of God-given gifts, not sure what we will open or unwrap or what will unfold with every moment, we will reimagine our definition of surprises and quite possibly see them as the Godly miracles that He intended all along.

Daily Scriptures
Monday
Ephesians 2:10 "For we are God's handiwork, created in Christ Jesus to do good works, which God prepared in advance for us to do."

How does reimagining myself as God's handiwork and masterpiece change the way I approach my day, my life, and my interactions with others (including myself)?

Tuesday
Ephesians 3:20 "Now to him who is able to do immeasurably more than all we ask or imagine, according to his power that is at work within us,"

How does this verse reimagine what I believe God is able to do in my life?

Wednesday
Isaiah 43:19 "See, I am doing a new thing! Now it springs up; do you not perceive it? I am making a way in the wilderness and streams in the wasteland."

Does this verse help to reimagine new opportunities in my life? How can I apply this verse to my day today?

Thursday
Jeremiah 29:11 "'For I know the plans I have for you,' declares the Lord, 'plans to prosper you and not to harm you, plans to give you hope and a future'."

What does this verse mean to me? How does knowing the Lord's good plans for my life reimagine my thoughts today?

Friday

Psalm 139:7 "Where can I go from your Spirit? Where can I flee from your presence?"

How does this verse reimagine my thought life, knowing there is nowhere I can go today that The Holy Spirit is not with me?

Weekly Wrap Up

Reimagine redefined:

How can I apply this to my daily life?

Week
44

Redo

Redo

Verb
Definition – to do something over again, to make again
Synonym – duplicate, reprise

When I was a little girl, I loved playing games with my dad. We would shoot basketball, play miniature golf, and boards games. Playing mini golf was one of my favorite games, especially when we went on family vacations to the beach. Whenever I would miss my putt, I would shout "do over" and hope my dad would let me redo my shot. Surely I would do better the next time. My sweet dad would let me grab my golf ball, replace it where it had been and redo my putt. Sometimes I improved, and sometimes I did not, but I was always grateful for the opportunity to have another chance. My precious dad was always great at allowing me the possibility of improving my score and making me smile. Getting to have a redo on my putt allowed me to learn from the first putt, how the slope made the ball break. It gave me useful information for the next attempt. This was valuable information that my dad instructed me to use when I tried my "do over" putt. If not, it was just another wasted shot.

When it comes to our daily lives, we get as many "do overs" and redo's as we need. With God, when we mess up, sin, or think we have done something so incredibly wrong that there is no way God can forgive us, we simply go to Him, confess our sins, and He is faithful to forgive us. He gives us a redo. Just like in mini golf, when we miss the hole, sin is defined as a failure to miss the mark—breaking one of God's commandments. Since none of us are perfect, we will not hit every shot we take, or make every putt in life. We all need a redo. We all need a second, third, or 100th chance. And God is faithful to give us another chance when we come to Him, confess our mess ups, and ask for another chance or a redo. He will give us as many "do overs" in life as we need.

Lamentations 3:22-23 says, "The faithful love of the Lord never ends! His mercies never cease. Great is His faithfulness; His mercies begin afresh every morning." What a great promise! We get a redo every morning and a fresh start every day. We get the chance at a new start each and every morning. Yesterday is in the past and we cannot do anything about it but learn from it. Just like the putt on the mini golf course where my dad would teach me to learn from my first attempt, we need to learn from our past. We need to learn from what we did the day before that did not work. Maybe something we did worked, and we can build on that knowledge too. We should ask ourselves every morning, what are we going to do with our fresh start? How am I going to use my redo today? Are we helping someone who may be in the same situation or place that we were in this time last year or before we knew God? We have been given this new start and redo for a reason, so how are going to use it?

Do not sweat small starts. God has placed dreams, purposes, and plans within each of us. These plans and dreams are all individualized and catered to the gifts and talents He has given each of us. In order to fulfill these plans and purposes, it will take hard work, prayer, and determination, but the sense of accomplishment will be overwhelming. But we need to start somewhere. We need to begin right where we are, doing what we are doing. We may think it is too late for us, but God is giving us a redo and today is the day. Ask yourself what can you do today to accomplish what you need to accomplish in the next year? In the next five years? We get a chance at a redo today, so take complete advantage of it. Do not sweat small starts. By taking baby steps today toward redoing what you could have or should have done yesterday gets you one step closer to achieving your goals. If you have a big dream, start today, right where you are, making a difference with the fresh start and redo that God has given you. He has given you the chance to move your golf ball, learn from the first putt, and play the twists, turns, and slopes again with the hope of getting closer to the mark. Why not take advantage of the redo and make the most of a fresh start—what better time than today?

Daily Scriptures
Monday
Isaiah 44:22 ESV "I have blotted out your transgressions like a cloud and your sins like mist; return to me, for I have redeemed you."
What does this verse mean to me?

Tuesday
Zechariah 1:3 "Therefore tell the people: This is what the LORD Almighty says: 'Return to me,' declares the LORD Almighty, 'and I will return to you,' says the LORD Almighty."
How can I return to the Lord again today?

Wednesday
Psalm 23:3 "He restores my soul. He leads me in paths of righteousness for his name's sake."
How has God restored my soul and how do I need to remember this truth today?

Thursday

Isaiah 57:15 ESV "For thus says the One who is high and lifted up who inhabits eternity, whose name is Holy: "I dwell in the high and holy place, and also with him who is of a contrite and lowly spirit, to revive the spirit of the lowly, and to revive the heart of the contrite."

How does this verse help me today?

Friday

Luke 22:31-32 NLT "The Lord said, 'Simon, Simon, listen! Satan has wanted to have you. He will divide you as wheat is divided from that which is no good. But I have prayed for you. I have prayed that your faith will be strong and that you will not give up. When you return, you must help to make your brothers strong'."

How does this verse help me when I feel like I have failed, been broken, and doubted God's goodness again? Who in my life can I help that may be struggling to be strong, encouraging them to see God's goodness in their own lives?

Weekly Wrap Up

Redo redefined:

How can I apply this to my daily life?

Week
45

Refocus

Refocus

Verb

Definition – to put more effort into a particular activity

Synonym – transform, aim, point

Taking pictures has always been one of my favorite hobbies. I have scrapbooks filled with photos of my daughters growing up, family vacations, and trips. One thing that I have learned over the years of taking pictures is that the picture quality is determined by whether or not the images are in focus. I have taken my fair share of blurry photos. Trying to photograph moving toddlers is a difficult feat. Or if the person taking the photograph is moving, the images can be equally blurry. Either way, if the images are blurry, the picture quality is diminished.

The pictures of our lives tells the story we want to share with the world. We put many screenshots together to tell our story and sometimes those screenshots can be blurry. When projecting our stories on social media or in scrapbooks, we have the ability to delete the photographs we deem undesirable or not "post worthy." We can filter the image to project it in such a way that it only shows what we want others to see. We crop out people, backgrounds, and images that we don't want to share with others. We can capture several re-takes, if necessary, to get the perfect shot. Even with all the technology available to us, we cannot fix a blurry photograph. There is not a way to enhance, crop, or alter a fuzzy or unclear image. The participants and the photographer have only one option: to be still.

We tell the stories of our lives everyday through our words, actions, reactions, what we choose to say, and even what we choose not to say. These daily decisions are impacted by where we choose to place our focus. Just as in a photograph, there is a focal point that the lens needs to use in order to make adjustments. The camera lens is the apparatus through which the photograph is taken and it adjusts the amount of light that filters through it. The lens also has the ability to bring images closer or farther away, by zooming in and out, or magnifying people, objects, and places.

In our lives, our eyes serve as our camera lens. They filter in more or less light with the daily decisions that we make. With Jesus as our light, we have the ability to allow as much light into our lives as we want. We can make any adjustments necessary through what we choose to look at, what we choose to read, and what we choose to see. When we refocus our time, energy, attention, and priorities on God, then we allow more light into our lives. We also slow down and become still, allowing God to become our focus. When we are still, our lives become less blurry. Psalm 46:10 says, "Be still and know that I am God." Stillness allows for a clear picture of our lives to be seen and the haziness to be removed. When we refocus on God, our lens can also zoom in on God and bring Him closer. Our eyes magnify Him in the image of our lives and we then project Him on a larger scale to those around us.

We make these adjustments and refocus on God in our lives in several ways. Having a daily quiet time is critical to refocusing on God and His direction for our lives. My daily quiet time involves seeking His guidance every morning for my day, what He wants me to accomplish, and asking Him to focus my time and my priorities. I have a pen and paper and write down whatever He tells me. I refocus my attitude towards thanksgiving and gratitude for all that He has already given me. And I refocus on things above and remember that this world is not my home. I am just

238 - Cyndi Dodson

passing through. Maintaining an eternal focus allows for a perspective shift in how I deal with daily struggles and problems.

Some of us need to refocus our lives with God as the focal point in the picture. Our days and our lives have become blurry as they seem to roll one day into another, without any focus or direction. We can either be focused on the wrong thing at the wrong time or give focus to the wrong things for too much of our time. These things are called time stealers and we cannot let them distract us from the important things in life. Time stealers can be scrolling on social media, Pinterest, online shopping, anything that distracts us and keeps us unfocused. These things in moderation are not necessarily bad, but if they begin to take over our lives and cause things to become blurry, then it is time to refocus on what is important. Because what we focus on becomes larger in our lives, we have the choice of what we put in front of us. What we choose to zoom in on becomes closer, magnified, and larger in our lives. Some of these things can lead to feelings of negativity, or discouragement and are not helpful. But when we choose to refocus our time and attention to God, He comes closer to us. By making a few adjustments and filtering in His light, our lives become less blurry. When we are still in His presence, He is magnified for the world to see and there is no better picture than that!

Daily Scriptures
Monday

Proverbs 4:25-27 "Let your eyes look straight ahead; fix your gaze directly before you. Give careful thought to the paths for your feet and be steadfast in all your ways. Do not turn to the right or the left; keep your foot from evil."

How can I specifically refocus my eyes and gaze, giving careful attention to follow God's path rather than my own?

Tuesday

Colossians 3:23 "Whatever you do, work at it with all your heart, as working for the Lord, not for human masters,"

How can I refocus my attitude regarding my job to see that I am working for the Lord and not for human bosses?

Wednesday

Matthew 6:33 "But seek first his kingdom and his righteousness, and all these things will be given to you as well."

In what ways can I seek God's kingdom first in my life today?

Thursday

Ephesians 4:22-24 "You were taught, with regard to your former way of life, to put off your old self, which is being corrupted by its deceitful desires; to be made new in the attitude of your minds; and to put on the new self, created to be like God in true righteousness and holiness."

How can I refocus my attitude and my mind, putting on my new self daily in Christ?

Friday

Colossians 3:2 "Set your minds on things above, not on earthly things."

How can refocusing on things above help me worry less about earthly challenges in my life today?

Weekly Wrap Up

Refocus redefined:

How can I apply this to my daily life?

Week
46

Rebreak

Rebreak

Verb
Definition – to break again, to re-crack
Synonym – re-fracture

Many of us have had a broken bone or perhaps had experience with a child with a broken bone. I broke my arm when I was in kindergarten. Even as old as I am now, I still vividly remember the injury. I was having a great time playing on a seesaw with my friend on the playground at recess. My friend "bumped" me, which simply means when her end of the seesaw hit the ground and my end was up in the air, she bumped the ground extra hard. Typically the person on the lower end does not allow the seesaw to hit the ground, but she did, and I was not holding on to the handlebars tightly enough—I flew off the seesaw. Apparently it was extremely exciting as my mom came and took me to the emergency room for x-rays. I was filthy, covered in dirt from the playground and wet from the tears I had cried. I remember the pain as the x-ray technician moved my arm in several different positions to obtain the perfect image. Breaking a bone is quite painful. Being broken spiritually is quite painful as well.

In some cases when a person breaks a bone, after the cast is removed the injured bone has not healed in the way that the doctor has expected. The bone, even after being immobilized for several weeks, has not healed and is not ready to be moved. In these cases, the bone must be rebroken and immobilized again. If it is not healed correctly, then the bone will not be able to withstand future movement, will not be able to be used properly and will hinder development and progress. Placing the body part back in a cast will aid in the healing process.

In Luke 7, we read about a woman who has crashed a dinner party that was given in honor of Jesus. She had lived a sinful life, and we learn that she was a "woman of the night," as my mom would say. She was a prostitute. She stood behind Jesus, weeping and holding an expensive jar of perfume. It was so expensive that it was said to have cost her a year's wages. She was broken by an occupation that she was not only ashamed of, but obviously needed in order to survive. She took the money that she earned for a year and bought a jar of perfume, that most women at that time did not even wear and brought it to the party. She first wet Jesus' feet with her tears, then her kisses, and then broke the jar of perfume and poured out the contents on His feet. I can only imagine the sight. The guests at the party could not believe He as allowing such a sinner to touch Him. Jesus saw only her brokenness. He saw not only the broken jar of perfume, but He saw the brokenness of her life. He saw that the woman took the jar of perfume that cost a year of wages, symbolizing her past and she broke that and poured it out at His feet. She gave Him everything she had, broken, and poured out. That expensive perfume was her most prized possession at the time. It cost everything she had but it had to be broken in order to get past it. Sometimes we need to rebreak our past and pour it out at Jesus' feet so we can move forward in our lives.

This expensive perfume not only symbolized this woman's past, but it was her most prized possession. It cost all that she had at the time. What is our most prized possession? What are we holding onto? Our marriages, our past, our jobs, our future, our children? Some of these things we have broken before. We have put them in a cast or a sling in the hopes they would heal, but in reality they did not heal the way the Great Physician intended. We did not break them for God. They may have been broken by the world, by bad decisions, or by life. But they have never been broken at the feet of Jesus and poured out for Him.

Am I willing to break my most prized possession and pour it at the feet of Jesus? Before you answer, remember this: Jesus is heaven's most prized possession, and He was broken and poured out for you. So whatever it is that you think you are holding onto that is so valuable, I guarantee it is not more so than Him. Fill the earth with your sweet fragrance and pour out your love today by rebreaking your jar at the feet of Jesus.

Daily Scriptures
Monday
Psalm 51:17 ESV "My sacrifice, O God, is a broken spirit; a broken and contrite heart you, God, will not despise."

What does it mean for me to give God my broken, contrite heart? How does that look in my life today?

Tuesday
2 Corinthians 4:8-9 "We are hard pressed on every side, but not crushed; perplexed, but not in despair; persecuted, but not abandoned; struck down, but not destroyed."

How does this verse help me in times of struggle, knowing that although challenges may be all around me, I will not be crushed or destroyed?

Wednesday
Psalm 73:26 "My flesh and my heart may fail, but God is the strength of my heart and my portion forever."

What peace does this verse give me today?

Thursday

Isaiah 40:29 "He gives strength to the weary and increases the power of the weak."

What does this verse mean to my life today?

Friday

Lamentations 3:22-23 "Because of the Lord's great love we are not consumed, for his compassions never fail. They are new every morning;"

What does it mean to me today knowing that God's mercies are new every morning and His compassions never fail me?

Weekly Wrap Up

Rebreak redefined:

How can I apply this to my daily life?

Week
47

Re-grip

Re-grip

Verb

Definition – to seize hold of something again

Synonym – reclasp

I learned to play sports while growing up from my dad. He taught me how to swing a softball bat and a golf club. I am naturally predominantly right-handed but can use both hands fairly well, especially when it comes to sports. My dad is the same way, and he swings a golf club and a bat left-handed, so naturally I learned to do these things left-handed as well. One of the first lessons I learned is how crucial the grip of the bat and club are when it comes to your swing. Proper hand placement on the club is critical, as well as how tight or how loose one holds it. If you hold the club too tightly, then you can't swing effectively, your hands will ache, and you will not allow the club to do the work. If you hold the club too loose, then it will fly out of your hands. The first lesson is learning to grip the club or bat with the correct intensity. This allows the equipment to swing freely, creates the correct rhythm, releases the tension in your body, and ultimately creates the power and force needed to hit the ball. That's the fundamental goal in both golf and softball.

Similarly, what we hold onto in life and how tightly we grip it is just as important. Our grip on certain ideas, beliefs, people, customs, habits, thoughts, and behaviors ultimately determines how we learn, grow, and live. When we grip too tightly, it hurts when the Father pries our fingers loose and takes things from us according to Corrie Ten Boom. What we grip or hold onto can be any number of things: occupational status, a relationship that takes precedence over God, habits and addictions that keep us in bondage, a prideful mindset or even busyness. 1 John 2:15-17 says, "Do not love the world or anything in the world. If anyone loves the world, love for the Father is not in them. For everything in the world—the lust of the flesh, the lust of the eyes, and the pride of life—comes not from the Father but from the world. The world and its desires pass away, but whoever does the will of God lives forever." We are called to grip or hold onto the will of God and not things of this world. Our goals, dreams, past hurts, ambitions, intentions, attitudes, and perceptions are all things we are called to grip loosely.

If we re-grip and adjust what we hold onto, what are some things we can grasp onto in our lives? Romans 12:9 tells us, "Don't just pretend to love others. Really love them. Hate what is wrong. Hold tightly to what is good." These three instructions are central to adjusting our grip and holding onto what is important in life.

First, love should always be genuine. 1 John 4:8 "But anyone who does not love does not know God for God is love." Love is not simply an attribute of God, He is love. Our source of love comes from Him and being followers of God, we must love one another. A true believer, one who is saved and filled with God's love, must live and abide in love toward God and others. This love cannot be fake or a fake it until you make it kind of love. It is a love that naturally flows out of us to our family, friends, and yes, even our enemies. Jesus is our example of how to love one another. Our love should always be genuine, real, and sincere.

According to Romans 12, we should also hate what is evil. Sadly, we live in a world today that is surrounded by evil. What would have been done in secret just a few years ago is now done in public. We have public figures, Hollywood celebrities, athletes and politicians that are sympathetic to vile behavior and promote evil while mocking Christianity. They use their platforms, success, and voices to support causes that endorse hate, immorality, and wickedness. As Christians, we are called to hate evil. We are not called to hate the people, but the actions. This is not a new concept, however. There have been many believers before us that chose to stand up in the face of evil and not condone the actions of the wicked. Queen Esther stood up against Haman and saved the Jews, the prophet Elijah stood up against the heinous King Ahab for worshipping Baal, and Moses stood up against Pharoah and brought the Hebrews out from Egyptian slavery. We have historic examples to emulate as we unite and stand up against evil but in some cases it takes one person to take an initial stand. One voice, one heart, one soul that decides to hate what is evil and confront it head on. We are called to hate evil, not just dislike it. Not kind of avoid it. But to hate it. If you sort of dislike something, then you will allow that in your home or your life, and it will become part of your existence. If you say you hate cats, but get a kitten, then it grows up to be a cat and becomes part of your life. The same way with evil and sin. What you allow into your home and your life is what you are willing to have be a part of your being. If you hate evil or sin, you will not stand for it or allow it into your family or your home. In fact, you will rise up against it, just like the Bible greats of the past.

Finally, we are called to hold tightly to what is good. We need to regrip and grab ahold of the good things of this world. We may think we have a firm grasp on the good things in life, but having a big house, a great job, a sizable bank account, and fast car are not the good things in life. We must learn to see the world and define what is good through God's perspective. The choice between good and evil has been presented to people as far back as the garden of Eden. We are called to "seek good, not evil and then the Lord will be with us, just as He says He is. Hate evil, love good, maintain justice in the courts. Perhaps the Lord God Almighty will have mercy on the remnant of Joseph" (Amos 5:14-15). So what are the good things that we should hold to, according to the Bible? God is good (Mark 10:18). But we tend to evaluate our definition of His goodness based on our day, our feelings, or our mood. We calculate the goodness of others based on their "niceness" to us, their good manners, how eloquent they speak, or in modern times we look at how politically correct a person behaves. They are good if they fall in line, keep their mouth shut and do not "rock the boat." Perhaps they give money to the poor, say nice things about others, or hold the door open for people. But in reality, goodness is much more. It is the fruit of the Spirit that, as our character is transformed, we reflect God's nature in our lives. Goodness not only involves action, but true goodness requires a heart change as well. So, holding onto what is good, adjusting our grip, allows us to grab hold of what is genuinely good in this world.

Just as gripping the golf club and softball bat too tightly causes tension in our body, holding onto worldly things in our lives causes tension as well. It will produce pain and achiness in our hands and body. When we release our grip and hold things with the correct intensity, then the tools in our lives can work the way they are intended to work. They will be more efficient and effective, we can swing more freely, and create the correct rhythm in our lives. Ultimately, the driving force behind our movement and being is God. When we regrip and hold life the way He says, then it allows His power to work through us. Then we can accomplish the purpose and plans that God has for us and maybe hit the ball out of the park while we are at it.

Daily Scriptures
Monday

1 Thessalonians 5:21-22 "...but test them all; hold on to what is good, reject every kind of evil."

How am I holding onto what is good in my life and rejecting evil?

Tuesday

Hebrews 10:23 "Let us hold unswervingly to the hope we profess, for he who promised is faithful."

What does it mean for me to re-grip or hold onto the hope that I profess in Christ? What does that practically look like in my life today?

Wednesday

Hebrews 3:14 "We have come to share in Christ, if indeed we hold our original conviction firmly to the very end."

Do I firmly hold onto my convictions or do I waiver when situations become challenging? How might I stand more firmly moving forward?

Thursday

Proverbs 17:28 "Even fools are thought wise if they keep silent, and discerning if they hold their tongues."

How do I need to re-grip my tongue and watch my words?

Friday

Psalm 94:18 "When I said, "My foot is slipping, your unfailing love, Lord, supported me."

How has God held His grip on me and supported me when I have felt like I was slipping? How can this serve as a reminder in my life today?

Weekly Wrap Up

Re-grip redefined:

How can I apply this to my daily life?

Week
48

Renew

Renew

Verb

Definition – to restore something to its former state

Synonym – refresh, restore

Every few months I like to review my memberships and update any necessary information and passwords. It is a good time to evaluate and see if I have any memberships to unwanted or outdated ones that I no longer need. It is eye-opening to see how many memberships I have to applications, programs, networks, and programs. And more times than not, these memberships automatically renew without my need for authorization. My membership to Netflix, Amazon Prime, and Hulu just to name a few, automatically renew and do not need my permission or approval. These networks are streamed into my home and into my life on an automatic basis. I flip a switch and I can choose what I see, listen to, and allow into my home. But have I ever stopped to think that with the power of that switch, I am also choosing what I allow into my mind and into my heart? These platforms automatically stream, with the push of a button or the sound of my voice (if I want to get fancy or hi-tech), and they speak life or death, encouragement or despair, hope or doubt, faith or fear. And each time I tune in and watch or listen, I have to ask myself, what am I automatically pouring into my mind and my heart? Am I building my faith or tearing it down? I am not saying I cannot watch anything that is secular or does not preach the gospel, but I do need to be aware of what I am pouring into my mind.

Romans 12:2 says, "Do not conform to the pattern of this world but be transformed by the renewing of your mind. Then you will be able to test and approve of what God's will is—His good, pleasing, and perfect will." We hear people say, "I just want to do God's will, but I don't know what that is," or "I just wish God would tell me what He wants me to do." It all begins with the renewing of our minds and in order to renew our minds we must take God's word from our head to our heart. We cannot just blend in with the world if we want to be different from the world. We are called to stand out. We must apply His word to our hearts and our lives in order to live differently. We are useless Christians if all we do is blend in and conform to this world. Jesus did not blend in and we are called to not blend in either. In order to stand out, we must stand on His word, stand up for others, and stand in the gap for those in need. All of these things begin with a renewing of our mind and what we put into it.

Our minds are fallen, sinful in nature, and in need of transformation. Our actions, reactions, and responses all begin with our minds and our thoughts. If we can transform our minds, then we can transform our lives. If we change what we put into our minds, then what flows out will change as a result. Titus 3:5 says, "He saved us, not because of works done by us in righteousness, but according to His own mercy, by the washing of regeneration and renewal of the Holy Spirit." Renewal comes from the Holy Spirit. When His Spirit comes into our minds and bodies, what flows out of us is life change. It is not anything we do or deserve but it is all because of what He does for us. When we have filth and dirt in our minds, God has to work harder to get through all the grime to speak to us. He is always talking to us and telling us His good and perfect will for our lives. When we remove the clutter and debris and renew our minds, it opens up a clear pathway for Him to speak and for us to hear Him more distinctly. When we transform and renew our minds, it puts His word on auto-renew so that a membership to God's plan and purpose for our lives is fulfilled. His streaming device is always enabled with perfect connectivity, and I pray that His word and His plan is what I live by every day, with automatic renewal.

Daily Scriptures
Monday
Colossians 3:10 NKJV "...and have put on the new man who is renewed in knowledge according to the image of Him who created him,"
How can I be renewed by this verse today?

Tuesday
Titus 3:5 NKJV "...not by works of righteousness which we have done, but according to His mercy He saved us, through the washing of regeneration and renewing of the Holy Spirit,"
How does the Holy Spirit's washing renew me today? How can I ruse this verse to renew my words and actions today?

Wednesday
Isaiah 40:31 "...but those who hope in the LORD will renew their strength. They will soar on wings like eagles; they will run and not grow weary; they will walk and not be faint."
How does God renew my strength so I can soar like an eagle?

Thursday
Proverbs 11:25 "A generous person will prosper; whoever refreshes others will be refreshed."
How am I renewing and refreshing other people in my life?

Friday

Acts 3:19 "Repent, then, and turn to God, so that your sins may be wiped out, that times of refreshing may come from the Lord,"

What do I need to repent so I may be renewed in Christ? How does this refresh and renew me today?

Weekly Wrap Up

Renew redefined:

How can I apply this to my daily life?

Week
49

Realize

Realize

Verb
Definition – to impart new life or vigor
Synonym – re-energize, strengthen

I remember the day that my husband and I brought our oldest daughter, Taylor, home from the hospital. We were first-time parents and were overcome with excitement. Her delivery had been long, complicated, and difficult but we were overjoyed with the thought of bringing her home. My husband drove so slowly that I thought we would get a ticket for backing up traffic, but we finally made it into the driveway. We carefully unloaded her car seat and carried her into the living room. I tenderly set her down, still strapped safely in her car seat, in the middle of the living room and my husband and I looked at each, sat down on the couch and said, "Now what?" We both had feelings of doubt and uncertainty as what to do next. We had experienced all the birthing classes and read all the books about what to expect, but no one really discussed what to do with her once we got her home. We both thought something would "kick in" and we would automatically just know what to do next. He was looking at me and I was looking to him. We each had our own set of "what if" questions swirling in our minds but neither one wanted to ask the other one out loud. It was then that the doorbell rang, and my father-in-law came over with home-made hamburgers and broke the silence. He entered the room and began to act as if nothing had changed. Yes, there was a new precious life in the room, but everything else was still the same. My husband and I were now parents. We were able to continue moving and living but now with a new little member in our family. It was such a relief to realize that even though some things change, some things do stay the same.

In Exodus, we read about Moses. He had been called by God to lead the Israelites out of Egypt. God had spoken to Moses in a profound way – through a burning bush, but Moses was reluctant to heed God's call. In Exodus 3, God reassured Moses of who God is (Exodus 3:14) and told him exactly what to say (Exodus 3:15.) But still Moses doubts (Exodus 4:1), "Moses answered, what if they do not believe me or listen to me and say the Lord did not appear to you?" Have we not all been there? Have we doubted God? Will we admit it? God has been pretty obvious in what He has said to us or called us to do and yet, we still doubt Him. God continues to be patient with us, repeatedly, just as He was with Moses. Moses continued to resist the call on his life because he thought the call was dependent on his own abilities. Moses said in Exodus 4:10, "I am not eloquent. I am slow of speech and of tongue." Moses continued to argue with God (which is never a good idea if you think you are going to win) and kept telling God why His plan would not work (yet another bad idea). Moses still had his eyes fixed on his limitations, his faults, and his shortcomings, and he told God to send someone else (Exodus 4:13). I don't know about you, but I can relate to Moses. When Taylor was sitting in the middle of our living room floor all those years ago, I silently asked God, "What were you thinking? Surely you meant for someone more worthy, smart, eloquent, or capable to be her mom." My insecurities, fears, and doubts, thank God, did not keep Him from blessing me beyond measure. When I was faced with the mission of motherhood, I felt under-qualified, ill-equipped, and unworthy, but I am so thankful that is not what God saw. He did not see that in Moses either. And just as Moses had to realize, I had to come to realize that it is not about my strengths, abilities, or worth. It is all about the Great I Am. It does not matter who I am, but rather who God is. Whether it is leading a nation, raising a child, praying for a friend, starting a new job, or loving on a neighbor, whatever He has called you to, He will equip you to do it. Realizing that our ability to do what He calls us to do is found in Him and Him alone is where our strength lies. And He even blessed me with two more daughters after Taylor, all of whom I cannot imagine not having in my life. I realize they are actually on loan from Him, and I am just blessed to love and take care of them while we are here on Earth. I am thankful for God's provision and blessing and that I am not powerful enough to mess up His calling on my life. I am sure Moses felt that way too. And just as Moses had to realize that God was for him and promised to always be with him, we too need to realize that in our lives. When we realize that God is God and let Him be God, no one can stop His purpose or plans for our lives, not even us.

Daily Scriptures
Monday

1 Corinthians 3:16 "Don't you know that you yourselves are God's temple and that God's Spirit dwells in your midst?"

Do I truly realize that I am God's holy temple? How does this change the way I live my life today?

Tuesday

John 14:20 "On that day you will realize that I am in my Father, and you are in me, and I am in you."

How does this verse change my realization of my identity?

Wednesday

John 13:7 "Jesus replied, 'You do not realize now what I am doing, but later you will understand'."

How does this verse grow my faith and trust in Jesus today?

Thursday

Proverbs 16:9 "In their hearts humans plan their course, but the LORD establishes their steps."

How does this verse help me to realize God is in control of my life?

Friday

Jeremiah 17:14 "Heal me, LORD, and I will be healed; save me and I will be saved, for you are the one I praise."

How does this verse help me to realize God's power in my life?

Weekly Wrap Up

Realize redefined:

How can I apply this to my daily life?

Week
50

Realign

Realign

Verb
Definition – to restore to a former position or state
Synonym – readjust, reorganize

By the time my fifth grade year arrived, so had the time for me to finally be able to get braces. I was overjoyed and excited with the prospect of these shiny, metal brackets on my teeth. I was hopeful that my buckteeth or what my orthodontist affectionately called an overbite would be greatly improved. I was also hopeful that the huge gap between my two front teeth that I was certain a large bus could be parked between, would be fixed as well. The painstaking process of impressions began, and the braces were installed. I wore the braces for close to four long years. Four years of rubber bands, head gear, adjustments, wax for irritated gums and orthodontist cheek-ups, and four years of braces in school pictures and in life. Yes, my teeth were a mess. So when the time came for my daughters to get braces, and their excitement brewed, I did not attempt to squash their enthusiasm. The oldest daughter had absolutely no difficulty, but the middle daughter had more trouble than I thought possible for teeth. Through numerous teeth being pulled and not being born with eye teeth (whatever those are), and then needing bone grafts for implants, we had an ordeal with her mouth. Finally, the time came for our third daughter to get braces, and in true fashion for the last child, they have invented an amazing product just in time for her – Invisalign. These remarkable braces are clear aligners that are removable for eating; worn all the time, but never seen. These clear braces are the best invention, especially for the teenage population. Our youngest daughter went through the alignment of her teeth without anyone ever knowing she wore braces. It seemed that one day her teeth were suddenly straight, as if it had happened overnight. There were no metal "brace face" pictures. She was spared the grueling, public process of alignment.

But this not how change always occurs in life. This is not how alignment occurs in our daily lives. Sometimes we are spared the grueling, public agony of transformation, but more often than not, we get to experience modification through our own "brace face" events. Sometimes coming into alignment with God's will for our lives is ugly. Sometimes it is obvious on our face for others to see. It is worn on our smiles, our faces, on our words and on our lips for all those we encounter to see and hear. We feel the pain and the movement, the tugging of the head gear, the stretching of the rubber bands the irritation of the brackets – everything that God uses to bring us into alignment with His will for our lives. All of it is necessary to bring us into alignment where He needs us to be and to do what He has called us to do. Phil 1:6 says, "And I am sure of this, that he who began a good work in you will bring it to completion at the day of Jesus Christ." Although coming into alignment can be difficult or painful at times, we can always trust that God is doing the work, He loves us, and since He began the good work in us, He will bring it to completion. He will not leave us in our braces, unfinished, with a metal mouth.

I like to think of the process of alignment like the caterpillar that turns into a beautiful butterfly. The caterpillar actually stuffs itself with leaves and grows plumper and longer. It sheds its skin, and one day it just stops eating, hangs upside down from a leaf or branch, and spins a silky cocoon. While inside its protective chrysalis, the caterpillar begins to radically transform its body and eventually emerges as a beautiful butterfly. While most of the butterfly's change is invisible to others, the butterfly still goes through a painstaking process to come into alignment with what it was intended to be all along. The butterfly does not quit or give up along the way or halfway through the process of becoming a butterfly. Just as we may get stuck upside down, in a sticky situation or a tough time where we cannot see our way out, like the butterfly, we must hang in there. We need to go back to Phil. 1:6 and remember that God began a good work in us, and He will see it through to completion. His alignment, although not always pleasant or pretty, yields beautiful results. His ways are higher than our ways. His process is better than ours and ultimately, He will make our smile beautiful, one that will change the world.

Daily Scriptures
Monday

Philippians 1:6 "...being confident of this, that he who began a good work in you will carry it on to completion until the day of Christ Jesus."

Am I confident that God is completing His good work in my life? How does this promise change my outlook for today?

Tuesday

Joshua 24:15 "But if serving the Lord seems undesirable to you, then choose for yourselves this day whom you will serve, whether the gods your ancestors served beyond the Euphrates, or the gods of the Amorites, in whose land you are living. But as for me and my household, we will serve the Lord."

How can I choose today to serve God? What does that look like in my life?

Wednesday

Romans 12:2 "Do not conform to the pattern of this world but be transformed by the renewing of your mind. Then you will be able to test and approve what God's will is—his good, pleasing and perfect will."

How can I realign my thoughts with God's will for my life today?

Thursday

Matthew 6:33 ESV "But seek first the kingdom of God and his righteousness, and all these things will be added to you."

How can I realign my desires to seek God's and His kingdom first in my life today?

Friday

Proverbs 3:9 ESV "Honor the Lord with your wealth and with the first fruits of all your produce."

How can I realign my wealth today to honor God with my resources?

Weekly Wrap Up

Realign redefined:

How can I apply this to my daily life?

Week
51

Reject

Reject

Verb

Definition – to refuse to accept, turn down, to throw back

Synonym – decline, refuse

When I was a little girl, one of my all-time favorite movies was *Rudolph the Red Nose Reindeer.* At the time, it was only on television once a year, at Christmas. This movie could not be downloaded on a streaming platform, purchased on DVD or VHS, or even rented a Blockbuster. Those places and things were not invented yet. So every Christmas when the *TV Guide* showed that this special was to be aired, I would make a bowl of popcorn and watch every minute. The characters in this movie classic spoke to my little heart, but at the time I didn't understand why. It was not until I was older and somewhat wiser that I came to realize why I was so enamored with this movie.

The animated classic is narrated by Sam the Snowman and the story takes place in no other town but Christmastown at the North Pole. Rudolph is a baby fawn and has been born with this glowing red nose that no one has ever seen before. Santa arrives on the scene and declares to Donner, Rudolph's dad, that Rudolph will never make the sleigh team because of this abnormality. So Donner proceeds to cover Rudolph's nose with mud in hopes to hide this malformation. Rudolph tries several things to cover up his nose and eventually ends up leaving Chrismastown because he feels that his nose will endanger his family and his friends.

When Rudolph leaves he meets Hermey, a young elf who does not want to be an elf but wants to be a dentist, and their adventure begins. They travel to the Island of Misfit Toys. These are toys that are rejects and have some sort of strange quirk about them that supposedly no child would ever want to play with them. These toys include a water gun that squirts jelly, a train with square wheels, a bird that swims, a boat that cannot stay afloat, a spotted elephant, and a Charlie in the Box. These toys have been tossed aside and live together on Misfit Island. This part of the movie was always my favorite part. Looking back, I now realize why.

Each one of those toys feels as if it had something wrong with it. Each toy was a reject and did not feel as if it fits in with the other toys that it was made to be like. The train with the square wheels did not think it could roll correctly like his friends and the water gun actually squirted jelly. Maybe you can identify with these toys like I did and still do. You think you do not look like the other people around you. You do not roll through life like your friends as smoothly as it appears they do on a daily basis. Or perhaps what comes out of you is a little messier than those around you. What you say squirts out of your mouth before you have had time to filter it or maybe it comes out not quite like you intended for it to sound. Maybe what other people want you to be in life is not what you feel that you should be or are called to be. Like Hermey, you want to be something completely different than what your family has desired for you. You feel like a reject and that society has cast you aside, and although you may not be living on an actual island by yourself, you do feel isolated from others. Maybe you feel like the spotted elephant and your blemishes are so obvious that there is no possible way anyone could love you. You feel that you are covered in flaws, imperfections, and defects, and those are the only things that others see when they look at you. Maybe you are like the bird on Misfit Island that is supposed to fly, but instead you swim. You cannot seem to get off the ground. You do not even feel as if you can get above anything, and your circumstances keep pulling you down. Or possibly, you feel like the boat that cannot stay afloat. Like you are drowning, and life just keeps weighing you down. Like no one sees you. You keep going under, and everyone else is sailing and staying afloat. Just like these misfit toys, you feel out of place, like you do not fit in with the people around you. Perhaps you can relate to several of these "defects." But I have good news for you! God loves misfits. He loves the downcast, broken, and rejected. That includes all of us, whether we want to admit it or not. We are all broken in some form or fashion. If we were perfect, we would not need Jesus, and trust me, He is completely necessary for us all.

What we view as a defect in our lives can be the very thing that God uses to help others and draw them closer to God. God can use what we see as our deficiencies as the instrument that leads others directly to Him. Our weaknesses can point others back home. Take Moses for example. According to Exodus, his ineffectual speech was deemed by Moses as one of his greatest flaws. Moses argued with God that he could not be used by God to lead the Israelites because of this deficiency, but God showed him! Not only did God use Moses in spite of his flaws, but he also worked through that so-called limitation to prove to Moses that God is bigger and better than any and all our deficiencies. Our imperfections are what make us unique and if we were perfect, then Jesus would be unnecessary.

Paul uses jars of clay as an illustration in 2 Corinthians chapter 4 to describe how broken, flawed, and fragile we can be. "We now have this light shining in our hearts, but we ourselves are like fragile clay jars containing this great treasure. This makes it clear that our great power comes from God, and not from ourselves." These clay jars were something that the Corinthians could relate to as they were commonplace in their society. These jars had many uses from cooking to carrying water in their homes, so they were familiar with this description. Paul relates the fragility of these jars to how easily we too can become broken, how simply dropping or knocking one over would result in a jar cracking or shattering to pieces. Yet he reminds us that we are still of great use and value. Paul states that these cracks are how God's light that is within us is able to shine through to others. If it is not for the cracks, blemishes, and flaws, then God's light would remain unseen. We hold His light in us and through the brokenness of our lives, we are able to let Him shine. So if you can relate to a misfit or a broken jar full of cracks and blemishes, then that is when God is able to do His best work. In our weakness He is strong. He holds us together and through our imperfections, His perfect light shines even more brightly.

Daily Scriptures
Monday
Luke 10:16 ESV "The one who hears you hears me, and the one who rejects you rejects me, and the one who rejects me rejects him who sent me."

What does it mean to me that God would say this about me?

Tuesday
1 Peter 2:4 ESV "As you come to him, a living stone rejected by men but in the sight of God chosen and precious."

Have I ever been rejected by others? What does this verse mean to me and how can it help me when I feel rejected by people in my life?

Wednesday
Psalm 94:14 "For the Lord will not reject his people; he will never forsake his inheritance."

What does it mean to me to know that God will never reject me?

Thursday

Isaiah 41:9-10 "I took you from the ends of the earth, from its farthest corners I called you. I said, 'You are my servant'; I have chosen you and have not rejected you. So do not fear, for I am with you; do not be dismayed, for I am your God. I will strengthen you and help you; I will uphold you with my righteous right hand."

How can I use these verses at times when I may feel rejected by others?

Friday

Numbers 14:11 NKJV "Then the Lord said to Moses: 'How long will these people reject Me? And how long will they not believe Me, with all the signs which I have performed among them?'"

What does it mean to me to know that God has been and is still rejected in the world? How does this change the way I live my life and how I view rejection?

Weekly Wrap Up

Reject redefined:

How can I apply this to my daily life?

Week
52

Respite

Respite

Noun
Definition – a pause for relaxation, a short period of rest
Synonyms – break, recess, pause

I have been accused, on one or more occasions of talking too fast. Even with my slow, southern draw, I can begin to tell a story and before I know it, my speech and language is almost incomprehensible. It is no wonder I have raised three daughters who are exactly like me. I am constantly asking them to slow down or repeat what they just said as they are talking 90 miles per hour. I blame it on the fact that I have so much to say and if I do not include every detail quickly, then someone will tell me to just get to the point. In reality, I think I just talk fast, and I always have. I walk fast, possibly drive a little too fast, and I want things done yesterday instead of waiting patiently for them to happen. But that is not how God intends for us to live our lives. When we begin to speed too fast whether in our speech, decisions, or just life in general, God can build in commas that help us to breathe. Just as in a sentence, commas differ from a period. Commas are just a point in a sentence to take a breath and keep going. Commas are a brief pause, and unlike a period, they are not a complete end to a thought or direction. Many times in our lives we come to a place that is simply a comma, but we assume we are at a period. We are supposed to take a small pause or break and we end up thinking it is an end. God builds in these respite moments for our benefit so we can pause, catch our breath, and move on. These moments were in the Bible too.

In Psalms, the word "Selah" is used 71 times. Selah's actual definition has been discussed by many different scholars, but most agree that it deals with a pause in music or to reflect on what was just read. In either instance, the reader is instructed to take a breath and pause, like an overstated comma. I do not know about you, but there have been times I have read several pages of a book, even the Bible, and thought, what did I just read? My mind wondered, I read it way too fast, or I just did not understand what was being said. Even if there was a "Selah" written on the page, I probably would have ignored it. And I get that way with life too. I rush through an activity or event just to check it off my to-do list and hurry on to the next thing. I don't even realize that the activities and events I am rushing through make up the life that I am living. Then along comes God and places one of His profound "Selah" moments in my life to get my attention. What I may see as a period or a distraction, He is simply using as a respite moment for my benefit. These intentional pauses give us an opportunity to reflect on what is going on in our lives, maybe help us comprehend something we don't understand or keep our minds from wondering too far off track. Perhaps these respite moments give a chance to gain a little perspective in our lives. We can get so hurried in life that we lose all sight of God and His hand or voice in our lives. If we don't have the ability to put a Selah moment in our lives every now and then, He will help us.

It is in these pauses and respite moments when we meet with Jesus that He changes us. It is in the pause or being still that we can embrace "Selah." Psalm 46:1-11 says, "God is our refuge and strength, a very present help in trouble. Therefore we will not fear though the earth gives way, though the mountains be moved into the heart of the sea, though its waters roar and foam, though the mountains tremble at its swelling. *Selah* There is a river whose streams make glad the city of God, the holy habitation of the Most High. God is in the midst of her; she shall not be moved; God will help her when morning dawns. The nations rage, the kingdoms totter; he utters his voice, the earth melts. The Lord of hosts is with us; the God of Jacob is our fortress. *Selah* Come, behold the works of the Lord, how he has brought desolations on the earth. He makes wars cease to the end of the earth; he breaks the bow and shatters the spear; he burns the chariots with fire.'**Be still and know that I am God. I will be exalted among the nations; I will be exalted in the earth!**' The Lord of hosts is with us; the God of Jacob is our fortress. *Selah.*" This powerful Psalm uses the word *Selah* three times. It does not tell us to pause, try to figure everything out on our own, and try not to stress. It does not say, be still but continue to worry. It says to be still and know that He is God. Being still is an activity in itself. We are pausing our efforts and surrendering, letting go, and letting God be God. We trust and know that His ways are higher than our ways and we rest in the fact that no matter what is going on around us, He will be exalted among the nations, and we have no reason to fear.

These respite or *Selah* moments can seem unproductive, especially when we believe that we are the ones that are holding our worlds together. When we believe that the faster we talk or the quicker we get things done the better, and it all depends on our efforts, we soon realize that mindset is all an illusion. God is the only one who can hold the world in the palm of His hand. We may think we are the glue that is holding our lives intact, but in reality He is the one that keeps everything in it's place. So I invite you to create small *Selah* moments in your life. If you are not already spending a few minutes with God every day, start with 5-10 minutes in the morning. Be still and quiet. Read a few scriptures, starting in Psalms. Calm your mind and let Him quiet your heart as you find comfort in

His presence. He will amaze you with His peace as you begin to want to spend more and more time with Him. As your *Selah* moments grow and you find respite in His presence, there is no other place you will want to be: sitting still and knowing that He is God.

Daily Scriptures
Monday

Exodus 33:14 ESV "And he said, 'My presence will go with you, and I will give you rest'."

How can apply this verse to my life today?

Tuesday

Psalm 23:2 ESV "He makes me lie down in green pastures. He leads me beside still waters."

What does this verse practically look like in my life today?

Wednesday

Psalm 37:7 ESV "Be still before the Lord and wait patiently for him;"

How can I be still before the Lord today?

Thursday

Hebrews 4:9-11 ESV "So then, there remains a Sabbath rest for the people of God, for whoever has entered God's rest has also rested from his works as God did from his. Let us therefore strive to enter that rest, so that no one may fall by the same sort of disobedience."

Do I practice Sabbath in my life? If not, what needs to change to ensure that I do?

Friday

Psalm 4:8 ESV "In peace I will both lie down and sleep; for you alone, O Lord, make me dwell in safety."

How can I lie down tonight in God's safety and respite in His peace?

Weekly Wrap Up

Respite redefined:

How can I apply this to my daily life?

Bonus
Weeks

Relentless

Adjective

Definition – determined to do something without giving up

Synonym – persistent, constant

I could list numerous women who have impacted my life in countless ways and each of these women have several traits in common. They have inspired me to be a better wife, mom, and woman but most importantly they have encouraged me to seek the Lord and His face always. These women are my heroes of faith and I am grateful that God brought them into my life. As they compel me to love better, reach higher, grow deeper, and live freer, they ultimately inspire me to realize God's grace and power and to walk in His favor and anointing on my life. One of the primary characteristics that all of these women share is being relentless. That is a rare quality in

individuals, especially females, but I am so thankful that these ladies modeled this attribute in their lives. As I was able to watch this quality unfold in their lives, I could develop it in my life as well.

However, Jesus is the ultimate example of being relentless. The story in Mark 4 demonstrates Jesus being relentless, even if the beginning of the story may not appear so. Jesus tells the disciples beginning in Mark 4:35, "Let's go to the other side." A sudden storm develops, and the waves break over the boat, so much so that the boat nearly broke. Mark 4:38 continues the story, "Jesus was in the stern sleeping on a cushion." There was Jesus, in the storm on the stern or the back of the boat, sleeping.

To be stern (outside of boating terminology) means to be relentless, especially in authority, so He was already relentless just by being on the back of the boat and just by being Jesus. A boat is guided or steered from the back of the boat, usually by a rudder or a motor. Jesus, being at the back or stern of the boat, was already leading and steering the boat, even though He was sleeping. The disciples did not realize it. He knew they were headed into a storm, but He was at the stern and was relentless in His leading, guidance, and authority. His relentlessness was not only over their direction but over the storm as well.

The disciples did not realize prior to this encounter who Jesus was and even doubted His authority. They were just like the waves tossed on the ocean that James refers to in James 1:6 when he says that anyone who doubts is like a wave on the sea blown and tossed by the wind. But Jesus was peacefully sleeping in the stern of the boat, guiding them to a storm that He knew was coming. He was on the boat with them and was going to be in the storm with them and was not afraid. Jesus was about to reveal His power. The storm was necessary, the thunder, the lightning, the wind, and the waves were all necessary in order to reveal God's power. We may be frantically trying to alert Jesus about the storms raging in our lives, but He knows exactly what He is doing. It may seem like He is sleeping in the stern of our boat, but He is relentlessly working on our behalf. He is guiding, leading, and directing us to exactly where He has called us to be. We need to develop this characteristic in our lives as well. We need to be relentless in our pursuit of Him and His peace. There are times we need to lay down in the back of the boat and know He's got this, no matter what "this" is. A storm may be on the horizon, or we may be in the middle of one right now, but with Jesus in our boat we cannot lose. We need to pursue Him relentlessly and know that whatever is on the other side, it is always worth getting in the boat. When He says, "Let's go to the other side" that is not a suggestion. Jesus is making a promise. It may seem like, "Hey, let's go for a little boat ride" suggestion, but it really is a promise. He never tells us how we will get to the other side. That is where our faith comes in and that's where we are called to be relentless in our pursuit, trust, and hope in Him. Some days may be smooth sailing, bright sunshine, fun, laughter, and smiles. Other days may be

choppy water, dark skies, clinging to the side of the boat, seasick, with no land in sight. We do not get to decide how we get to the other side. We only get to be relentless in our faith in the One Who is steering the boat, speaking to the wind and the waves, and calming our fears. As we grow in our faith, our hope is that we can inspire and encourage others to become relentless in their lives as well. For what was once modeled for us as young believers, should be our goal to model for the next generation. As we look to Jesus as our ultimate guide, may we reflect His attributes so that others can see Him more clearly, and may we be relentless in that pursuit every day.

Daily Scriptures
Monday

Hebrews 10:39 ESV "But we are not of those who shrink back and are destroyed, but of those who have faith and preserve their souls."

How can I be relentless in my faith today?

Tuesday

Luke 18:27 ESV "But he said, 'What is impossible with man is possible with God'."

What looks impossible in my life right now but with relentless faith is possible with God?

Wednesday

Zephaniah 3:17 ESV "The Lord your God is in your midst, a mighty one who will save; he will rejoice over you with gladness; he will quiet you by his love; he will exult over you with loud singing."

What does it mean to me to know that God sis relentlessly singing over me with gladness?

Thursday

Psalm 23:6 "Surely goodness and lovingkindness will follow me all the days of my life, And I will dwell in the house of the Lord forever."

How does it change my day knowing that God relentlessly follows me with His lovingkindness and goodness?

Friday

Jeremiah 29:13 ESV "You will seek me and find me, when you seek me with all your heart."

How can I relentlessly seek God and live for Him today?

Weekly Wrap Up

Relentless redefined:

How can I apply this to my daily life?

Refine

Verb

Definition – to free something from impurities or unwanted imperfections

Synonym – purify, clarify

All three of my daughters have played volleyball at some point in their lives. My oldest daughter won a state championship in volleyball, and my middle daughter played travel volleyball. All three have played competitive beach volleyball. A fundamental concept in volleyball is learning that when a ball is passed over the net to a player, the player needs to "better the ball," which simply means to make a pass that improves the possibility of making a better play or making the situation better. The player should make a pass or improve the ball that was passed to them. It does not matter how hard, or how fast, or bad the pass was that came to them. The player's only job at that point is to improve the next pass. They are not to complain, pout, or make excuses about how lousy the ball was that was hit to them. They simply are to improve the play moving forward. My daughters have also learned that this concept coincides with life. I have taught them that they are to leave people and places better than they found them. I don't care if this is the place where you stop for coffee in the morning, your job, your bedroom, your job, or a stranger on the street. Whoever you encounter and wherever you go, you improve that person or situation just by having been there. If that means cleaning up the messy countertop at the coffee shop or picking up dropped clothes at the store, we should "better the ball" for the people and places we encounter on a daily basis. We should leave the places we have been better for our friends, family, co-workers, and even strangers. Even if we are passed a "bad ball" or a tough situation that may seem negative, we cannot pout, complain, or make excuses. We must work with the ball we are passed and do everything we can to make the situation better. And this is not possible in our own strength. We are not called to do any of this in our own ability or power. God promises us that we can do all things through Him who gives us strength (Phil 4:13) and he is working through us constantly, refining us daily.

As we are being refined daily, we can compare it to the silversmith who purifies silver and the process that takes place doing so. Malachi 3:3 says, "He will sit as a refiner and purifier of silver; he will purify the Levites and refine them like gold and silver." Several things happen when silver is refined with heat. The silversmith must hold the bits of metal in the hottest part of the flame so that the impurities will melt away. The debris will ruin the purity of the silver so the silversmith must skim off the lesser impurities until only the silver remains. The silversmith must stay close to the fire and his silver because if he leaves it in the fire too long, it can be damaged. Once all of the impurities have been burned and skimmed away, the metal becomes shiny and reflective, and the silversmith knows it is fully refined when he can see his reflection. It has been said that this process is similar to how we as God's creation are refined as well. The temperature of our lives has been turned up around us so high in order to burn away all the impurities and cleanse our character from contaminants. We are being improved by removing all the impurities, toxins, and poisons in our lives like bitterness, rage, jealousy, or lust. All the while we must remember that as the temperature rises, that God never leaves us. His hand is always on us so that we will not be in the fire too long and we will not burn. He is waiting just long enough so that we shine and reflect His glory and He can see His reflection in us. He knows that when the refining takes place, no matter what comes our way going forward, we will be able to handle life's flames. We have been through the refining and are stronger on the other side. When life passes us a "tough ball" we will be able to make a better pass for all those we come in contact with daily. We will not complain, pout, or make excuses but we will improve the situation for those around us. We have been refined and now shine God's reflection for all the world to see.

Daily Scriptures
Monday
Psalm 12:6 "The Lord's promises are pure, like silver refined in a furnace, purified seven times over."

What does it mean to me that God's promises are refined and purified? What does this look like in my life?

Tuesday
John 15:3 "You have already been pruned and purified by the message I have given you."

How have I been refined by God's message in my life?

Wednesday
Malachi 3:3-4 ESV "He will sit as a refiner and purifier of silver, and he will purify the sons of Levi and refine them like gold and silver, and they will bring offerings in righteousness to the Lord. Then the offering of Judah and Jerusalem will be pleasing to the Lord as in the days of old and as in former years."

What does this verse mean to me?

Thursday

Romans 8:18 ESV "For I consider that the sufferings of this present time are not worth comparing with the glory that is to be revealed to us."

How does this verse help me as I consider my current challenges in life?

Friday

Isaiah 48:10 ESV "Behold, I have refined you, but not as silver; I have tried you in the furnace of affliction."

Has my meaning of refining changed? Is there anything in my life that I feel God is refining and removing?

Weekly Wrap Up

Refine redefined:

How can I apply this to my daily life?

Response

Noun

Definition – a reaction to a question

Synonyms – answer, reply

Life can be challenging. I know on several occasions, I have wondered and even asked, *where is God?* It seems like evil is winning, life is out of control, and I cannot seem to get my feet under

me before another wave of chaos hits my life. We turn on the television or look at our news feed on our phones and read about another devastating disaster in our world, and wonder what is next. Or perhaps the disaster is a little closer to home. We open our eyes and before our feet hit the floor in the morning, we consider the day ahead and all of the challenges, financial struggles, family problems, work worries, health concerns, and overall life worries. We are overwhelmed with anxiety and worry before we even get out of bed. What is our response? How do we respond to all of the trials that are thrown our way? Are we supposed to catch every ball that is thrown at us? Are we required to answer every one of life's questions? If so, what is our response?

There is a tiny book of the Bible that offers some insight into some of these questions and more. Habakkuk was also troubled with the world around him. He was concerned about the moral decay of his world and the spiritual decline of the society in which he lived. Sound familiar? He cried out to God, even complained to Him about what he was feeling. (Habakkuk 1:2-4) Also sound familiar? God's response to Habakkuk troubled him even more. God was actually going to use the evil nation of Babylon to punish Judah. (Habakkuk 1:6) Habakkuk was not only uneasy about God's reply and plan, but he also complained to God... again. (Hab. 1:12-17) This pattern may not sound familiar to you, but it really speaks to me.

Habakkuk begins to learn, and we all can learn from him. He learns a new response — he learns to rely on the steadfast faithfulness and love of God, because he realizes he can trust in Him. Even though Habakkuk could not understand, see, or conceptualize God's plan, he trusted God and lived by faith knowing that His ways are higher than our ways. When we live this kind of faith-filled life, we cannot help but rejoice in Him.

We all know someone who never seems to be happy or content with what they have or with their life in general. Their favorite phrase is "I'll be happy when..." or "I would be content if ..." and then fill in the blank with – when I get married, when I lose 10 pounds, when I get a promotion, when I go on vacation, when I get a bigger house, when I save more money, when I have a baby, when I retire. Meanwhile, life is passing them by while they are waiting for life to be wonderful. When we put "if" or "when" as determinants for our happiness, then we are making our circumstances determine our joy. The truth is that things, people, places, and circumstances will never bring true, lasting joy. The things listed above may happen and that is great if they do. But if they do not, we need to determine ahead of time that life will be joyful in spite of our circumstances. That is what Habakkuk learned and that is what we should learn from him.

Circumstances should not dictate whether we are happy, content, upset, angry, peaceful, joyful, or kind. The events that happen in our lives cannot be controlled, but only our response to them. Habakkuk's response, confident declaration, and prayer in verses 17 and 18 of chapter 3 is a beautiful expression of his faith in God indeterminant of his circumstances. He realized that this world is not his home. God can use even wicked people like the Babylonians to fulfill His

purpose and we can trust His plan for our lives no matter what. We can trust His timing to be perfect (Hab. 2:3) "For the revelation awaits an appointed time, it speaks of the end, and it will not prove false, though it linger, wait for it; it will certainly come and will not delay." God can use evil people at inopportune times to complete what only He can do in our lives. What we see as delays and unpleasant, such as our interactions with wicked people, can be just what God has orchestrated and planned all along. We simply need to trust in His faithfulness and goodness. We do not need to worry about our circumstances and how God will come through or when. We simply need to trust that He will, in ways that only He can.

In Habakkuk 3:17-18, he finishes his writings with some final, profound thoughts. "Though the fig tree does not bud and there are no grapes on the vines, though the olive crop fails, and the fields produce no food, though there are no sheep in the pen and no cattle in the stalls, yet I will rejoice in the Lord; I will be joyful in God my Savior. The Sovereign Lord is my strength; He makes my feet like the feet of a deer; He enables me to tread on new heights." Habakkuk has a lot going wrong in his life. But the astounding word in these verses is "yet." Although the list of what is wrong in his life is lengthy, Habakkuk is able to surmise that God is his strength. I think we should write our own version of verses 17-18. Perhaps your list looks a little different than Habakkuk's, you are not concerned with your lack of sheep or cattle in the pen or perhaps you are. But write your own version of the last two verses of Habakkuk in your own words. Tell God again or maybe for the first time what worries you in life. Tell Him what you are anxious about before your feet hit the floor in the morning. He already knows but it is good for you to write it down and see it on paper. Share with God your anxious thoughts, but do not forget the most important part. Do not forget to include your "yet" statement. Tell God that although you are worried, concerned, and anxious, yet I will trust in You. I will trust You, God, and your timing. I will trust You to come through in my life at the perfect time, using who You to choose to use and how You choose to do it. Write your own version of Habakkuk 3:17-18 and then sit back and watch God work. Prepare to be amazed as He responds to you and answers quite possibly with Habakkuk 1:5, "Look at the nations and watch and be utterly amazed. For I am going to do something in your days that you would not believe even if you were told." When we trust God with our lives, He amazes us with His response.

Daily Scriptures
Monday

"A gentle answer turns away wrath, but a harsh word stirs up anger."
How can I make my responses today gentler?

Tuesday

Romans 8:31 "What, then, shall we say in response to these things? If God is for us, who can be against us?"
How does this scripture change my response to life's challenges today?

Wednesday

Colossians 4:5-6 "Be wise in the way you act toward outsiders; make the most of every opportunity. Let your conversation be always full of grace, seasoned with salt, so that you may know how to answer everyone."
What do my responses to unbelievers look like in my daily life? What needs to change so my responses demonstrate the love of Christ?

Thursday

Psalm 34:4 "I sought the Lord, and he answered me; he delivered me from all my fears."

How has God responded to my cries and delivered me from my fears?

Friday

Proverbs 15:23 "A person finds joy in giving an apt reply— and how good is a timely word!"

Do I give timely words to those around me in my daily life? How can I do this more?

Weekly Wrap Up

Response redefined:

How can I apply this to my daily life?

Reflect

Verb

Definition – to think back, deliberate

Synonyms – contemplate, consider, ruminate, ponder

In order to see ourselves, we must look to "see" our reflection in a mirror or in a body of water. Our image reflects to us. We never actually see ourselves unless we look in a mirror. We can see parts of ourselves, such as our hands, our feet, or our legs. But we can never see our faces unless we see a reflection viewed through a mirror or a picture. We can't see our own face without it being a reflection or being reflected to us. What we see is determined by what we are looking at and where we are looking. This thinking sounds obvious, but it is foundational for our lives. Sometimes we get caught up and spend more time looking at our reflection, concerned with our appearance, rather than looking around and seeing what really matters. We are more concerned with what the world sees in our outer appearance and what we see in the mirror rather than what Jesus sees in us and what we should see all around us. We put an emphasis on our reflection in the mirror and what our outer reflection looks like to the world, but what matters most is what Jesus sees when He looks at us. Now I'm not saying we can't look in a mirror, take care of ourselves, or care about our reflection. But our reflection will change when we look at our same appearance through the eyes of Jesus and begin to see ourselves the way Jesus sees us.

There are two different ways to see and look at things in our lives. We can glance, or we can stare. A glance is a quick, brief, or hurried look at something, whereas a stare is a more prolonged, fixed gaze. When checking our reflection in a mirror, we need to glance. Stares should occur when we are focused on our future. We should stare at the world around us with a heavenly focus.

So when we do look in the mirror, and our reflection doesn't look the same as it did, maybe 5, 10, or 20 years ago, when we see we're beginning to have a few more gray hairs, our skin is beginning to sag, or we have a few more wrinkles than we did just a few years ago, we need to ask ourselves a few questions.

1. *Is the image we see of ourselves, our reflection, the true version of ourselves? Are we pretending to be someone that we aren't, or does the world see our true, authentic identity?*

2. *Does the reflection that we see in the mirror reflect what God sees and what is reflected into the world? When Jesus looks at us, He sees beauty, purpose, freedom, courage, forgiveness, a warrior, blessed, confident, anointed, favored, peaceful, powerful, chosen, worth dying for, and priceless treasure. He sees Himself when He looks at you.*

3. *As our reflection changes and we age, are we just growing older, or are we growing wiser and maturing in Christ? Are we growing and producing more fruit?*

4. *When we reflect on our past, do we judge our past mistakes weighted with what we know today, or do we see God's hand of mercy, grace, and redemption? When we look at our past, it's important that it's only a glance, like looking in the rearview mirror of a car. We only need to take*

a quick glance back to see how far we have come in order to help us move forward.

5. *When we reflect on our past, do we see all the times that God has been there for us? Do we see His hand in our lives, how He has rescued us, saved us, and used us for His divine calling and purposes in our lives?*

6. *Has Jesus changed my reflection? When I look in the mirror, do I see all the things listed above? Do I see Jesus? Do others see Jesus when they look at me?*

7. *Do I feel seen? Do I realize that Jesus sees me? Do I realize that Jesus sees all of my hurts, pain, joy, prayers, and praises?*

8. *Am I using my reflection to change others?*

9. *Am I reflecting Jesus to the world around me?*

10. *If not, what can I begin doing today to see Jesus in my reflection, and then how can I begin to reflect Him to the people in my life?*

Redefine:

Conclusion

In Acts 5, the apostles were performing so many miracles, signs, and wonders in Jesus' name that men and women from all over brought the sick into the streets so that at least Peter's shadow would fall on them when he walked by. It was believed in those days that even a good man's shadow contained healing power. So how is a shadow made? When the sun shines on a person, he or she creates a shadow on the people and places around them. When the sun, Jesus the Son, shines His light on us, we create a shadow, touching those around us. Our shadows are our influence and the impact we have on others, and we cast them every day, sometimes without even realizing it. I have been fortunate to have had many people cast shadows on my life and impact me in tremendous ways. I had many wonderful teachers including Mrs. Thomas who touched my life, and she may not even remember me or realize how she impacted my life as her 4th grade student. I have had other people whose shadows have impacted my life negatively as well. Although the negative shadows have taught me powerful lessons in life, I choose to focus on the positive shadows and their subsequent life lessons.

We all have the opportunity every day to cast a shadow and impact the lives of the people and places around us. It can be as simple as a smile, an encouraging word, a compliment, a much-needed pat on the back, or simply holding the door for someone as they walk into a store. Or it could be taking the time to listen when someone's world is crumbling, fixing a meal when they are sick, holding their hand when a spouse has just walked out, or watching their kids for a couple of hours when they desperately need a break. The shadows we cast are the result of the Son shining on us and reflecting His light on the world around us. If all we do is absorb His light and never let it impact our world, then we have missed the point.

A Redefined life requires us to cast positive shadows, change the world around us, and make a difference for the glory of God. We need to ask ourselves how we are defined? Am I a Re-Defined woman of God? And if so, how am I casting shadows that impact this world for Christ? What difference am I making that will matter for eternity? Others are watching, listening, living within the proximity of our shadows, and observing our lives. May we live a Re-Defined life and may it always leave a shadow that points others to heaven.

Author Bio:

Cyndi Dodson

Cyndi is passionate about sharing the love of Jesus! She joyfully proclaims God's truth so that women can experience His unwavering faithfulness, undeniable peace, and uncompromising power in their everyday lives.

Married to her husband, Chris, for over 30 years, Cyndi is the proud mother of three amazing daughters, and a newly added son-in-love.

Cyndi holds a Masters degree in Counseling; she also teaches and speaks at women's events and writes an inspirational blog, all centered around one simple yet powerful message: Jesus loves you. Cyndi's deepest desire is for women everywhere to know and believe in the goodness of God.

She is author of *Finding the Me in MomM*e, and *ReDefined*. You can reach Cyndi through *MosaicMinistries.net* or at *CyndiDodson.net*.